I0037693

The Doctor of Business Administration:

Taking your professional practice to the next level

Publisher's Note

Every possible effort has been made to ensure that the information contained in this book is accurate at the time of going to press. The publishers and authors cannot accept responsibility for any errors or omissions, however caused. No responsibility for loss or damage occasioned to any person acting, or refraining from action, as a result of the material in this publication can be accepted by the editors, the publisher, Business Science Institute or any of the contributors or supporting organisations.

First edition published in the United Kingdom in 2022 by Ideas for Leaders Publishing, a business of IEDP Ideas for Leaders Ltd.

Apart from any fair dealing for the purposes of research or private study, criticism or review, as permitted under the Copyright, Design and Patents Act 1988, this publication may only be reproduced, stored or transmitted, in any form or by any means, with the prior permission in writing of the publishers. Enquiries concerning reproduction should be sent to the publishers at the following address:

Ideas for Leaders Publishing
42 Moray Place
Edinburgh
EH3 6BT
www.ideasforleaders.com
info@ideasforleaders.com

ISBN
Paperback   978-1-915529-00-8
Ebook   978-1-915529-01-5

© Business Science Institute and contributors
© Ideas for Leaders Publishing, 2022

Cover design: www.nickmortimer.co.uk
Typesetting: Sopho Tarkashvili;
www.linkedin.com/in/sopho-tarkashvili-a21499172

CONTENTS

AMBA & BGA: An Overview 7

AMBA Perspective of the DBA 9

Foreword 11

Introduction 15

PART 1: WHY THE DBA? 21

Chapter 1. The DBA as a Response to the Market 23

Chapter 2. The DBA and PhD in Business:
History, Similarities and Differences 33

Chapter 3. Why Choose the DBA Over a PhD? 45

Chapter 4. Turning the DBA to Your Advantage:
Opportunities and Challenges for Self, Organisation
and Wider Society 57

Chapter 5. Lifelong Learning in an Ageing Society:
the DBA as the New MBA 71

PART 2: THE DBA PROGRAMME 81

Chapter 6. DBA Candidate Profiles and Motivations 83

Chapter 7. Different Cultural/Geographical Motivations .. 95

Chapter 8. DBA Programme Design 103

Chapter 9. Partnership Between the DBA Supervisor
and Student: A Special Relationship 115

Chapter 10. Student Support in a DBA Programme 127

Chapter 11. The Supervision Relationship:
Working Through Differences in Priorities Between
Academic and Management Practice 137

Chapter 12. The Gains of Moving Online for a
Professional Doctorate 153

PART 3: THE IMPACT OF THE DBA 167

Chapter 13. Purpose and Creation of Community
in a Professional Doctorate 169

Chapter 14. Professional Development and Impact 183

Chapter 15. DBA as Identity Space 193

Chapter 16. The DBA as a Game Changer:
A Case Study from One Institution 205
Chapter 17. Communication and
Dissemination of Impact 215

REFERENCES 227

AUTHOR PROFILES 233
Helena Barnard 235
Claire Collins 236
Joy Garfield 237
Ruben Guevara 238
Helen Higson 239
Vassili Joannidès de Lautour 240
Michel Kalika 241
Drikus Kriek 242
Jane McKenzie 243
Michelle Mielly 244
Diego Norena-Chavez 245
Chris Owen 246
Emma Parry 247
Stephen Platt 248
Vivienne Spooner 249
Simon Willans 250
Nicky Yates 251

CONTRIBUTING INSTITUTIONS 253

ASTON UNIVERSITY BUSINESS SCHOOL 255

BUSINESS SCIENCE INSTITUTE 256

CENTRUM CATOLICA GRADUATE BUSINESS SCHOOL ... 257

CRANFIELD SCHOOL OF MANAGEMENT 258

THE GORDON INSTITUTE OF BUSINESS SCIENCE 259

GRENOBLE ECOLE DE MANAGEMENT 260

HENLEY BUSINESS SCHOOL 261

IEDC-BLED SCHOOL OF MANAGEMENT 262

AMBA & BGA: An Overview

The Association of MBAs and Business Graduates Association (AMBA & BGA), founded in London, UK in 1967, is the world's leading authority in postgraduate management education, business school accreditation and alumni/student membership. AMBA and BGA operate as two parallel accreditation and membership systems under the umbrella of AMBA & BGA. The key statistics for AMBA & BGA include:

290 business schools worldwide hold AMBA accreditation, including 11 institutions that have received AMBA accreditation for their Doctor of Business Administration (DBA) programmes.

Over 200 business schools worldwide hold institutional BGA membership (with some of them additionally holding BGA accreditation or BGA validation).

Over 60,000 alumni and students worldwide are individual AMBA members.

Over 5,000 alumni and students worldwide are individual BGA members.

Of the 290 AMBA-accredited schools, 116 hold Triple Accreditation (AMBA, AACSB and EQUIS) as of March 2022.

Business Graduates Association was the original name of AMBA & BGA from 1967 to 1989, after which the organisation was renamed Association of MBAs (1989-2018) and since 2019 has the combined name of AMBA & BGA. AMBA accreditation typically covers the MBA/EMBA portfolio of an institution but can also encompass the rest of the postgraduate generalist management education portfolio: the DBA and MBM/MSc Management/MSc Entrepreneurship programmes. BGA is a whole-school accreditation system focused on impact and sustainability.

I am pleased to highlight in this book DBA-focused chapters by eight of the leading AMBA-accredited business schools in Europe, Africa and Latin America. I wish these world-class DBA programmes and their DBA participants and DBA graduates continued success.

Andrew Main Wilson

Chief Executive
AMBA & BGA
London, UK

AMBA Perspective of the DBA

A Doctor of Business Administration (DBA) programme offers experienced managers an opportunity for advanced studies, allowing them to put their considerable practical experience in the context of theoretical knowledge, and to work on expanding the frontiers of practice in their field. Typical DBA candidates already hold a prior management degree, such as an MBA or another Master's, or a professional qualification. In their DBA theses, they very often aim to solve practical problems, most often applying research techniques and drawing data from their own organisation or industry.

The AMBA accreditation criteria define the DBA as a research-based qualification designed to make a contribution to the enhancement of transdisciplinary professional practice in management disciplines, in addition to a contribution to knowledge via the development and application of theoretical frameworks, methods and techniques. A DBA places emphasis on the novel application of theory, as well as the potential creation or testing of theory within the context of practice.

In this book, eight well-known business schools from different countries outline the perspectives of their DBA programmes. All of these programmes are AMBA-accredited. Thus, AMBA has analysed their DBA programmes against its detailed accreditation criteria and has awarded its prestigious accreditation after rigorous scrutiny by a panel of experienced academics.

Readers who consider pursuing a DBA will learn why the degree typically takes four years or longer to complete, and how the objectives and focus of a DBA differ from a PhD. The detailed description of the DBA programmes shows why the DBA is a lynchpin that brings together academia and industry. The book demonstrates that a DBA is an asset in global management education. This is why AMBA started accrediting DBA programmes in 2006, and this is why anyone interested in learning more about the unique characteristics of a DBA should read this book.

Bodo B. Schlegelmilch, Ph.D., D.Litt., Ph.D. (hon.)

Chair of the Board of Trustees of the Association of MBAs and Business Graduates Association (AMBA & BGA), London, UK; and Professor and Chair of the Institute for International Marketing Management, WU Vienna University of Economics and Business, Vienna, Austria.

Foreword

Jean Bartunek, Robert A. and Evelyn J. Ferris Chair Professor, Carroll School of Management - Boston College.

Entering a doctoral programme is always a big commitment, and clearly anyone considering doing so wants as much insight as possible about the potential career advantages and challenges involved. I have been aware, for some time, of professional doctoral programmes in the US, and often been a bit mystified by their classifications and purpose. They have many different titles (comparatively few are called DBAs) and quite diverse expectations of those who join. Their students have varied expectations of the kinds of roles a professional doctorate prepares them for. So sometimes they opt for the right doctoral programme, and sometimes the fit is not so good. Some participants do not even realise that their training differs compared to that of a PhD student, which can lead to resentment and confusion if their work is undervalued in academic circles by full-time academics dedicated primarily to theoretical and conceptual rigour with less concern for practical relevance. Such incoherent understanding can be divisive, sometimes unfortunately leading professionals to denigrate the types of academic research PhD students are trained to do.

So, I am very grateful to Jane McKenzie, and to Michel Kalika and Stephen Platt, the editors of this AMBA book for introducing me to the world of accredited DBAs, where a professional doctorate is carefully designed to encourage students to take their business and management practice to the next level without compromising the quality of the research. The book has taught me that, in the UK at least, and then, as I am learning, in Europe, South Africa and other parts of the world, there can actually be a coherence in professional doctoral education and a guide for faculty involved in it. Not only can there be a coherence, but the outcomes of the DBA might produce graduates who make significant contributions which, although different from a PhD, are still vitally important for developing leaders and managers capable of fostering organisation and ecosystem development in the broadest sense of that term. To the editor and authors of the chapters of this book: Thank you.

This book does an exemplary (and sorely needed) job of addressing crucial questions about development on a DBA. It lays out differences between a DBA and PhD and some of the advantages of investing this sort of professional doctorate (Collins and McKenzie), considers the profiles and motivation of typical students (Joannidès de Lautour). It sketches out for faculty the expectations for guiding and advising students, at least in the UK system (which focuses much more on individual and peer relationships between students and faculty than do US-based programmes, even PhD programmes). Thus, it teaches not only students, but faculty, what they are getting into when they participate in a DBA programme (e.g., Higson & Willans).

At a time when the impact of scholarly research is of crucial importance in virtually all professional fields, the book also does a very fine job of sketching out the types of impact that DBA students might achieve, perhaps even in collaboration with PhD trained academics. This is a valuable contribution in itself.

Consider just a few major contributions from the book, at least from my perspective. The editors Kalika and Platt help us understand where the DBA fits into the overall doctoral market. Guevara and Norena-Chavez, and Collins and McKenzie provide us with a brief historical perspective on the DBA that gives a clear sense of why the programme can be a worthwhile educational alternative choice compared to a classical PhD, particularly for professionals seeking to differentiate themselves after the MBA (Mielly and Joannidès de Lautour) by deeply investigating the complex problems encountered in practice. Parry and Yates help us understand the way programme design helps DBA students achieve both rigour and relevance in their research. Barnard provides a reflexive perspective on the design of a DBA programme in South Africa, and by doing so shows that programme design itself can evolve flexibly based on particular circumstances (with COVID certainly being one of them, as another chapter by Barnard shows).

Some chapters (e.g., Garfield; Collins and McKenzie) show how a DBA programme (at least in Europe) may involve as much individual contact with a supervisor as a PhD programme does. The importance of that relationship is not to be underestimated. In addition, the chapters in section two highlight the value of community support from fellow DBA students that is a distinctive part of DBA programme design (Yates and Parry, Barnard and Spooner). Several chapters highlight the professional development value of the DBA for future and current leaders and business executives (Kriek, Owen and others), which is a message of hope in a changing world. In another chapter, Barnard and Spooner argue for the importance of DBA training for implementing evidence-based management, which is a critical link between academia and practice that is further enhanced through effective dissemination of the knowledge generated (Kalika and Platt). Importantly, the case study of Higson and Willans shows that students, organisations and business schools benefit from the DBA.

Finally, as we all are aware, there are profound needs in our world for responding to global crises and challenges. Some of the chapters, (such as that by Kalika and Platt) show how those trained in DBA programmes may be particularly suited for enacting thoughtful responses to such challenges.

All in all, I found this book enormously informative and useful. I am not aware of anything quite like it in the US, but professional doctoral programmes in the US could certainly benefit from its insights.

If you, the reader, have any inclination to investigate professional doctoral programmes and their possibilities, I encourage you to read this book and learn from it. You will find in it a comprehensive, thoughtful, and stimulating perspective on the value that managers, leaders, organisations and indeed business schools can derive from engaging with a DBA.

Introduction

Michel Kalika, Business Science Institute

The Doctorate of Business Administration (DBA), a doctoral programme for managers initially created by Harvard in 1953, is destined for the same rate of development the executive education market for MBA programmes witnessed from the 1990s until today. From an emergent and niche market, the DBA programme will undoubtedly grow to answer the new needs of managers in increasingly complex and uncertain work contexts that require decision-makers who are trained in the critical thinking skills provided by a DBA programme for professionals.

This book has been written by professors and managers working in AMBA DBA-accredited programmes on three continents. It aims to explain why this development will happen, and why more and more managers will decide to pursue what is a rather special and specific doctoral programme. It also aims to answer many of the questions that future DBA students are likely to ask.

The book has been specifically written for practising managers, future DBA students, higher education journalists, HR managers, national higher education quality assurance agencies, ... aiming where possible to encourage the reader to explore the topic in more detail and further spark their interest in the DBA.

There are a number of reasons why DBA programmes could be about to begin a phase of unprecedented growth.

- The first reason is to do with the evolution of the level of training of managers. For several decades, Masters and MBAs in management have been expanding across the world, but they are no longer an element of differentiation in terms of career development. In large and international organisations, and in consulting firms, the DBA is becoming the new calling card for career progress.

- The second reason comes from the need for managers to think differently and to adapt new business models to meet the challenges they face. In order to find the solutions to deal effectively with the consequences of climate change, the digitalisation of the economy, health crises and geopolitical troubles, the off-the-shelf knowledge readily available on the internet is no longer sufficient. Managers need the time, the space and the tools to step back and to rethink their practice, guided individually by academic experts.

- The third reason is more of a personal one. An increasing number of MBA-qualified managers, very often with over 15 years of senior leadership experience, feel the need to reconsider the way they manage their life, and to give it a new sense of purpose with the ultimate aim of then giving their career a fresh direction. The DBA offers such an opportunity.

All the DBA programmes accredited by AMBA have their own specific features, depending on their country contexts and their own institutional history, for example. However, each of these internationally recognised programmes shares some key characteristics.

- Firstly, the DBA programme is a doctoral-level programme designed and structured specifically for practising managers. This means that these DBAs are part-time and adapted to the constraints of busy managers. DBA participants very often come to the programme with significant experience and expertise, and they come with a very clear idea of what their research topic will be. A topic that is generally focused on their current area of practice or experience.

- Secondly, the DBA programmes that are behind this book share common standards of quality and academic rigour. As AMBA-accredited programmes, they offer participants a guarantee of quality at a national and international level. In an emergent education market, accreditations are a key consideration for applicants. The quality of a DBA programme is mainly based on invisible characteristics (quality of the research process, responsiveness of the faculty, ...), which means it is often difficult for candidates to separate "the chaff from the wheat" and to distinguish the robust DBA programmes from the weaker ones. It is the role of accreditation bodies to help make this distinction clear. High-quality DBA programmes involve a research question explored through a review of the literature, research methodology, data collection and an analysis of the results that enables the practitioner-scholar to formulate managerial recommendations.

- Thirdly, and this point is a distinctive one compared to other doctoral programmes, at the end of a process that is embedded in management practice, the researcher will return to their area of practice to generate impact. There can be no DBA thesis without managerial recommendations that in turn are likely to make a significant contribution to the practice of managers, the performance of their companies and to wider society.

More generally, we can say that the DBA contributes to reducing the age-old gap between the worlds of practice and academia.

Of course, situations are different depending on the country. In the UK, the programmes from Aston[1], Cranfield* and Henley* were created respectively in (2001, 1999, 1992). In France, GEM* was the first-ever institution to create a DBA programme in 1993. At Paris Dauphine University in 2008, the author of this introduction developed the first DBA programme to be run in a French university. Business Science Institute*, in Luxembourg created its own DBA programme for managers in 2013. Since then, numerous programmes have been created in French-speaking Business Schools. In South Africa, Gordon Institute* welcomed its first cohort of students in 2012. In Slovenia, Bled School of Management's programme* dates from 2018. And the DBA programme at CENTRUM Católica* in Peru, dates from 2002.

This book has been structured into three logical and inter-related parts. The first part answers the question **Why a DBA?** The second part then describes the content of **the DBA programme,** followed by a third part that focuses on the **impact of the DBA.**

In part one, **"Why a DBA programme?",** the authors answer some important questions. They explain that DBA programmes exist to answer the need of the market, and clearly expose the differences between a DBA and a PhD. The authors provide the reader with reasons to choose a DBA over a PhD, and as such describe the specific features of a DBA that bring about an advantage for managers. Finally, the reader is invited to consider how the DBA might indeed become the new MBA in a very near future.

In part two of the book, **"the DBA programme",** the authors open up the black box of DBAs clarifying participant profiles and motivations, programme design, the partner-

---

[1] AMBA accredited DBA programmes.

ship between student and supervisor, student support mechanisms, the all-important supervision of the thesis, and what the gains might be of moving online for DBA studies -a recent and game-changing development in higher education.

In part three, **"the impact of the DBA"**, the authors discuss the huge added-value of a DBA for practising managers, their employers, and also wider society. Comparisons are once again made between the DBA and the traditional PhD, but this section also explores how academic institutions can benefit from the presence of a DBA in their programme portfolio, bridging the gap between the world of practice and education. This part also addresses questions related to the purpose and creation of community in a professional doctorate, professional development and the impact of DBA, the DBA as identity space, the social impact of the DBA, and how the DBA is becoming a game changer in the area of higher education. Last but not least, the communication and dissemination of the impact generated by the DBA is discussed, offering the reader new perspectives on the ultimate purpose of professional doctorates.

I cannot end this introduction without thanking all my colleagues who participated so joyfully and efficiently in bringing about this book. A special mention goes to Nicholas O'Regan from Aston Business School, who kindly accepted to review a number of chapters and played an active role in all the book steering committee meetings. I would also like to thank the AMBA team for their trust and support, especially George Iliev, Director of Strategic Projects and Innovation, without whom this project would not have gone ahead. My gratitude also goes to Stephen Platt from Business Science Institute for his efforts in coordinating the project.

Part 1

Why the DBA?

1

The DBA as a Response to the Market

Michel Kalika and Stephen Platt, Business Science Institute, Wiltz, Luxembourg

This chapter provides the reader with perspectives on how the DBA is a response to an emerging and increasingly prevalent executive market need for continuing professional development of a different nature to that offered by short courses designed for senior managers and business leaders.

Keywords: Market demand, DBA life cycle, DBA versus PhD, knowledge production.

Introduction

The creation of a Doctorate of Business Administration (DBA) by academic institutions occurs mainly in response to market demand. To illustrate this point, let's begin with a short personal story. Along with a number of colleagues, during the 1980s and 1990s we had been designing and running Executive MBA programmes for managers in numerous countries across the world. After some time, a few years after graduation, these now senior managers started to regularly get back in touch with us to discuss opportunities for pursuing their management studies. As a reader interested in this topic, it won't be hard for you to understand that when a professor has been teaching marketing and strategy all their life, this sort of relevant and interesting demand is rather difficult to ignore! Because the traditional PhD was ill-adapted to the requirements and expectations of these senior managers, who above all did not want to become full-time academics, we took the decision to create the first-ever Executive DBA run by a French university[1]!

What is a DBA?

A Doctorate of Business Administration is a doctoral-level programme intended for professionals who wish to carry out research to prepare a management thesis based on their professional experience (Kalika, 2017). This rather basic definition requires a number of additional comments to help the reader grasp the true nature of the DBA:

- The DBA is a programme involving both taught components and research, run by professors with the relevant experience and academic expertise to teach face-to-face or online seminars to senior leaders, and to carry out high-quality, personalised and sustained supervision of equally experienced and expert practitioner-scholars.

- The DBA is a doctoral-level third cycle programme, i.e., a post-second cycle Master's (including, post-MBA) programme which generally lasts between 3 or 4 years as is usual in Europe for doctoral studies in the context of the three-cycle degree structure (Bachelor, Master's, Doctorate) system. It carries 180 ECTS (European Credit Transfer System) credits, and is the highest academic qualification. For readers who are

---

[1] Programme created in 2008 and still running. Business Science Institute was subsequently created in 2013 to satisfy an increasing international demand.

potential DBA applicants, it should be noted that it is not possible to prepare a DBA thesis of the required standards in less than three years.

- The DBA is a programme that culminates in the presentation (or defence) of a written thesis, which is a substantial piece of written work. The qualification of 'Doctor of Business Administration' is awarded following the successful public defence (or viva) before an examination panel. In this sense, the DBA cannot be compared to Bachelor's or Master's programmes where graduation relies primarily on the acquisition of knowledge, understanding and other skills tested mainly by written exams. In the DBA process, the thesis and its oral defence are the centrepiece of the pedagogical process.

- A DBA thesis is an original written piece of work, addressing with rigour and relevance a management theme grounded both in the experience of the DBA student as a management practitioner and based on extant academic literature. It is for this reason that DBA students are commonly referred to as 'practitioner-scholars', or 'manager-researchers' given the importance of the confrontation between academic and management expertise. The DBA thesis is the primary result or output of the doctoral process, and contributes to the production of new knowledge. It is important to emphasise that a DBA thesis should not be a mere description of managerial practises or just a compilation of the academic literature; it should result in the creation of knowledge leading to the formulation of managerial recommendations that can actually be used by managers. This last point is the main difference between a DBA and an MBA programme, the latter focusing on learning through knowledge transfer.

- DBA programmes are more often than not designed as part-time study programmes, adapted to the constraints of practising managers, who enrol on the programme to take a step back from their practice and confront a 'problem' from their work (or a topic of particular personal interest) with the input provided by academic experts in the field of the student's research topic.

Why does the market need a DBA now?

The DBA is an answer to two types of latent demand coming from the market and more specifically from managers and business leaders.

The first type of latent demand is related to the personal motivation of practitioners. The development over recent decades of Master's and MBA programmes has meant that a large number of practitioners are qualified with this kind of degree. By way of illustration, according to AMBA, in December 2021 there were over 60,000 MBA graduates from AMBA-accredited institutions alone, of which there are just 300 in the world! After many years of experience, these managers feel the need to take their reflective thinking further, to step back from their work, and to take some 'quality' time to think deeply about their managerial practice. This need is also linked to the desire to improve their own management performance, and to transfer their experience and know-how, which very often takes the form of tacit knowledge that is not always easy to externalise, since it is embedded in action, procedures and routines. Moreover, the banalization, and some would say commoditization, of the MBA means that the

DBA is increasingly considered by senior leaders as a key distinguishing feature on their CV, particularly regarding access to C-Suite positions in international companies or organisations. Indeed, in some countries a doctoral qualification level is considered to be a prerequisite for access to senior executive positions. We can say that the DBA offers a solution to answering a range of managers' personal needs, namely: personal realisation through reflective thinking, recognition by 'standing out' in the employment market, transfer of expert know-how through the research process itself, publications, and a wide variety of other opportunities for sharing knowledge (see Chapter 17: 'The Communication and Dissemination of Impact').

The second type of latent demand is related to the modern-day world of management, which is characterised by a highly disruptive context. There is no need to remind the reader of the impact of the Artificial Intelligence revolution, the galloping digitalisation of whole parts of the global economy[2] (Kalika, 2000), the complex challenges raised by climate change, and more recently the effects felt by the worldwide COVID-19 pandemic. These events have raised awareness of the need for the business world to develop innovative ways of thinking and critical frameworks to be able to generate new business models. Our belief is that in such a 'wicked' (Rittel & Webber, 1973) context, a mix of business and academic expertise is required to imagine such a new way of thinking. The DBA is an opportunity for experienced managers and professors to work together to answer this global challenge across different organisational, industrial, and cultural realities.

---

[2] Something we called "e-management" 20 years ago.

How does the DBA generate impact for managers, organisation and society?

The observation of the disconnect between traditional management research and the real world of practice is now widely shared, as is the belief there is a need for research that is useful to managers, organisations and society. The DBA can reduce this gap in a number of different ways, as follows.

- The main purpose of DBA research is generally not to publish in academic journals[3], thus perpetuating the much lamented 'publish or perish' dilemma. On the contrary, the main purpose of a DBA thesis is to develop relevant reflective thinking that is grounded in theory as well as managerial experience, and to formulate recommendations that ultimately create impact. In this way, the DBA thesis can almost be considered as a "PhD++", since it adds managerial, organisational and societal impact to conceptual thinking. This is indeed the perspective adopted by AMBA when considering academic institutions for accreditation of their DBA programmes.

- The research topic is brought to the DBA programme by the manager, and will stem from a long experience in business or other categories of organisation. Because this topic is grounded in managerial practice, issues and real-world challenges, the expectation is that the outputs of the DBA research process will feed back into practice, generating impact.

- A successful thesis process depends on a regular, sustained and close interaction between the doctoral

---

[3] DBA programmes can have different objectives with regard to this.

candidate and their supervisor(s). This interaction is a way of reducing the gap mentioned previously between academic research and the world of practice. This point is crucial, since the supervisor will need to understand and acquire the tacit knowledge of the manager in addition to their own explicit research knowledge of the topic in order to guide the DBA student successfully through the research process.

- The research methodology used in the DBA thesis is increasingly based on the embedded collection of data (Chevalier et al., 2019), made possible as DBA students are themselves grounded in the real world of the organisation[4].

- A chapter dedicated to managerial recommendations stemming from the thesis findings, and which potentially generate impact beyond the immediate confines of the research process are also very often compulsory in a DBA thesis. These recommendations might concern the organisation where the manager works, its industry, and even wider society. For example, an analysis of the DBA thesis topics of graduates from Business Science Institute in December 2021, showed that just under 50% had a direct link with the United Nations Sustainable Development Goals[5], including categories such as: Quality Education (SDG4), Decent Work and Economic Growth (SDG8), Industry, Innovation and Infrastructure (SDG9), Reduced Inequalities (SDG10), and Peace Justice and Strong Institutions (SDG16).

---

[4]Qualitative approaches and Grounded Theory approaches are well adapted to DBA research. See for example: https://www.groundedtheoryonline.com/helen-scott/. Pr. Helen Scott teaches on our DBA programme.
[5] https://www.un.org/sustainabledevelopment/sustainable-development-goals/

- Last, but not least, the managers defending their thesis occupy positions in companies, in public organisations, or in government bodies where they have sufficient organisational influence to be able to implement their recommendations for positive change. For example, among the DBA graduates from Business Science Institute, one is the Prime Minister of an African nation, and two others hold ministerial positions. The case of consultants is also very interesting in terms of dissemination of research findings. For example, one of our DBA graduates based in France working on the external transfer of SMEs, developed a methodology that is now used successfully for all his clients, and has been developed into a formal training programme.

The considerations mentioned above explain why the DBA is a source of value creation, directly related to the impact that a DBA thesis generates.

An example of a response to market demand: the case of Business Science Institute

The idea that the DBA is an answer to the needs of the market is widely shared by the DBA programme actors we encounter from different countries, and especially those involved in this book project. In this final section of the chapter, we will use the example of Business Science Institute to illustrate how this market demand has been met since our creation in 2013.

- Professors with experience in the executive education field observed that traditional PhD programmes run by universities were not always adapted to the expectations of practising managers nationally and internationally. They therefore decided to create a DBA programme for managers from scratch.

- They also observed that DBA research topics were extremely diverse by nature, and required an equally wide range of specialised competencies in terms of faculty human resources. They therefore decided to create a network organisation able to integrate a broad selection of professors specialised in a variety of different management topics, and able to accommodate different research methodologies (e.g., quantitative, qualitative, deductive, inductive, grounded, action research, etc.).

- An increasing number of managers explained that their personal and professional constraints, or their geographical location meant it was impossible to participate in the face-to-face seminars organised during intensive week-end workshops. We therefore decided (prior to the COVID-19 crisis) to make video recordings of all taught components, and to develop a well-structured remote research progress seminar system attended by all members of the cohort.

- Because even the best distance learning formats generate barriers, our students (and faculty) continue to feel a need for interpersonal contact and interaction. We therefore decided to develop an annual event in Europe called the 'International Week', attended by our entire academic community in the last week of September, and where a variety of events take place (research presentations, thesis defences, conferences, alumni events, committee meetings, alumni meetings, graduation ceremony, etc.).

- Because language can be a barrier for managers, the seminars and courses that were initially taught in French are now also organised in English and German.

- Finally, because the DBA market is emergent and very different to the PhD market, the structuration of what our professors expect from their doctoral students was necessary. We therefore created a collection of books that clarify how to manage a DBA thesis. Books have been published on such topics as the DBA thesis project, on DBA research methodology, on data processing, etc[6].

Conclusion

For the reasons mentioned above, we consider that in the future the DBA could become the 'new MBA' in terms of growth rate. Of course, the DBA market will never reach the same size as the MBA market in terms of students, but we will see more and more managers qualified with a Masters or an MBA degree contemplating the perspective of enrolling on a DBA programme. However, given the resource-based and mindset challenges faced by many traditional universities for running successful DBA programmes, the higher education market may see the emergence of more alternative providers such as Business Science Institute in order to satisfy market demand.

---

[6] The DBA Thesis Project in Practice; Research Methods for the DBA; Discovering New Theories; Doctors Advising Doctoral Students; Let your Data Speak; Qualitative research. https://www.editions-ems.fr/livres/collections/business-science-institute.html

2

The DBA and PhD in Business: History, Similarities and Differences

Rubén Guevara and Diego Norena-Chavez, CENTRUM Católica Graduate Business School, Pontifica Universidad Católica del Perú

The purpose of this chapter is to present a brief review of the history of universities, the doctorate, the origins of the PhD, and the DBA. It also covers the main similarities and differences between a DBA and a PhD in business.

Keywords: History of universities, doctorates, PhD, DBA, business.

A brief history of universities

Universities are institutions of higher learning that have existed, in their modern form, since the onset of the second millennium. Europe is generally seen as the birthplace of universities, but as Peters (2019) stated: "the university as a form of organisation was peculiar to medieval Europe but there were organisational forms of higher learning peculiar to India, China, and the Middle East that considerably predate the European form" (p. 1063). He added that most lists of the oldest universities exclude the institutions of higher learning that existed much earlier than those in Europe. He made a well-documented description of the main ancient institutions of higher learning, different than today's university, that existed in ancient China, ancient India, and the ancient Arab world. The University of Al-Karaouine in Fes, Morocco is generally regarded as the world's oldest continually operating university. It was founded in 859 as a leading university in the natural sciences. Al-Azhar, another "university" located in Egypt, can be regarded as the second oldest.

Talking about universities as we know them today, Malden (1835) explained that "the oldest universities of Europe sprung up in the twelfth century, and were formed by the zeal and enterprise of learned men, who undertook to deliver public instruction to all who were desirous of hearing them" (p.2). These European universities taught mostly theology, medicine and law. The oldest institution of higher learning in Europe is today's University of Bologna, which was founded in 1088. The University of Paris and the University of Oxford, as institutions of higher learning, were both founded in 1096. The university as we know it today, with the necessary variations to adapt over time, originated when Pope Innocent III established the regulation of the institutions of the universities in 1215. The term "university" was applied for the first time to the Parisian school (University of Paris)" (p. 10). Malden (1835) explained that not only was the University of Paris one of the oldest universities in Europe, but also that it was the most famous and the most frequented of them all, with many universities throughout Europe copying its format and customs.

A Brief History of the Doctorate

The use of doctor to refer to a teacher also dates back to the twelfth century, having been introduced at the

Universities of Bologna, the University of Paris and the University of Oxford, likely from around the year 1151. However, even though the doctorate at that time was part of higher education, "the appellation had nothing technical in it" (Malden, 1835, pp. 16-17).

Starting in the year 1229, after Louis IX of France confirmed all the privileges conceded to the University of Paris by former kings, the doctoral degree was regularly granted to all the faculty members after a solemn examination, very much as it is done today. However, universities at that time did not carry out research, which means that doctorates were "awarded as an acknowledgement of one's ability to teach, not .... ability to research" (Jones, 2018, p. 818). So, the doctorate was initially conceived as a license to teach (*docere*), but it has evolved over time to become the highest academic degree granted by universities, focused above all on the ability to conduct research.

A Brief History of the PhD

The degree of doctor of philosophy originates in Germany, at the University of Berlin, where the old doctorate was reengineered during the first decade of the nineteenth century, with a new emphasis in research (Jones, 2018). Several European universities soon offered the new research doctorate created in Germany: Pierre and Marie Curie University in France in 1810, University of Paris (Sorbonne) in 1811, and the University of Zurich in 1833 (Simpson, 1983). This new approach to the doctorate had an impact across the world, becoming the gold standard for aspiring academics from across the US and most of Europe. The original doctorate therefore changed "from being a professional doctorate serving to benefit the individual's profession, to being a doctorate which established the student as a teaching professional in academia" (Jones, 2018, p. 816).

Nevertheless, Germany and several other countries in Europe now offer doctoral degrees that are equivalent to the PhD, but using other denominations, such as the doctorate in natural sciences *(Dr. rer. nat.)* or the doctorate in political science, business and economics *(Dr. rer. pol.)*. This is not a situation that is exclusive to Europe. *Stricto sensu,* in most non-English speaking countries the doctor of philosophy degree is only granted in the field of Philosophy. In all other fields they follow a practice similar to that in Germany: even though the degree granted is equivalent to a PhD, they are called in ways that reflect the specific disciplines they focus on.

The PhD degree (and its equivalents) is awarded when an individual has demonstrated the ability to carry out academic research and to produce new knowledge. It can be granted in any field of specialization, from the humanities, and any scientific discipline. Therefore, it can be awarded in history, philosophy, mathematics, physics, biology, business, medicine, and so on. Furthermore, it is a degree that is highly focused on research in a specific field, with the intention that the professionals who completes it truly master that particular subject. The degree is called *Philosophiae Doctor* due to the Greek roots of the word *philosophia,* which means "love of wisdom".

The first PhD degree in the US was launched at Yale University in 1861. Other American universities, such as Harvard, Michigan, and Pennsylvania also started to offer PhDs soon thereafter. In the UK, Oxford University was the first institution of higher learning to offer the PhD in 1914 (Jones, 2018). However, even before then higher doctorates such as the DSc and DLitt had been introduced in Britain by the Universities of London, Edinburgh, Oxford and Cambridge during the 1870s (Parks, 2005).

A Brief History of the Professional Doctorate

Professional doctorates are much newer than the PhD. They are designed to meet the needs of professionals who are not necessarily interested in teaching and/or research, but who want to complete a doctorate, while maintaining a strong link with students' present or future practice. These doctorates focus on research with a tangible use in the real world. They can take many forms, because they respond to the needs of the professional area in which they are conferred. Examples of fields in which professional doctorates are offered include Business Administration (DBA), Education (EdD) and Engineering (EngD).

These professional doctoral degrees provide an alternative avenue to the PhD, and are found especially in the Anglo-Saxon world, notably in the United Kingdom, Australia, the United States and Canada. Harvard University was the first to grant a professional doctorate in education in 1921 (Jones, 2018). This degree is a taught doctorate in a professional discipline, rather than in an academic area like the PhD is, and even though it is a research-based degree, the emphasis is on application within the student's professional practice (Huisman & Naidoo, 2006).

There is general agreement that the professional doctorate brings together academia, the student, and their area of practice. Malfoy and Yates (2003) talk about the professional doctorate occurring at the intersect between the university, the student's profession and the particular worksite of the research through the implementation of a hybrid curriculum. Fink (2006) depicted the professional doctorate as consisting of three intersecting ovals, where their union represents the professional doctorate. The professional doctorate is therefore devised for present or future practitioners, and the PhD for academics.

Main Characteristics of the DBA

The DBA is a professional doctorate that focuses on contributing to the professional practice in business administration and management, which means that students enrolling in this degree must already have experience in business.

The number of DBA programmes on offer proliferated especially in the 1980s and 1990s: in Australia there were more than 15 of those programmes in the early 2000s, while in the UK there were more than 40. They are less common in the USA where fewer than 10% of AACSB international accredited business schools offered a DBA (Banerjee & Morley, 2013). The first DBA was offered by Harvard University in 1953 (MacLennan et al., 2018).

The DBA focuses on applied research that addresses real-world organisational and business problems. It is a terminal, research-based degree, often part-time, that usually requires coursework, and a thesis. The thesis has to be based on empirical evidence and has to provide evidence of independent study, although the research topic tends to be focused on solving a practical problem rather than a theoretical one. Graduates will usually continue to work for companies, rather than in academia, even though some may also prefer to teach. Indeed, some graduates continue to work in practice while teaching in higher education.

Main Characteristics of the PhD in Business

The relative prevalence of the PhD in business versus that of the DBA varies across business schools and universities. As with all PhD degrees, the PhD in business is based on academic research, it is typically taught full-time and students usually continue with the degree after completing a Master's degree (rather than after gaining practical experience). This is because students' primary purpose is typically to become academics. Presently, some business schools prefer to run Executive PhD programmes, which is a sort of blend between a PhD and a DBA: it is part-time, mostly focused in developing advanced research competences, and to master a specific field of endeavour, but it is focused on top-level executives who want to continue in business.

Entry requirements are very demanding in both options, similar to other PhD programmes and involve an entry examination. Applicants are required to have a Master's degree, often in any field of study, typically with the argument that the PhD will in any case require a revisiting of the chosen area up to Master's level and beyond. Proficiency in English is required and typically research rather than business experience. Graduation requirements usually include the publication of one or more research papers in well-known journals, a thesis defence, and mastery of research methods and analytical methods, e.g., qualitative or statistical techniques. As in the case of the DBA, it is a terminal degree.

Similarities between the DBA and PhD in Business

In a nutshell, the DBA and PhD in business have a number of similarities and differences.

The most common similarities include:

- it is the highest university degree a professional can achieve.
- both have very demanding entry requirements.
- both usually require a Master's degree.
- both are research-based degrees.
- both require the appointment of a high level, experienced, specialized advisor or supervisor.
- most programmes involve coursework.
- both programmes last between three and four years.
- both degrees demand a lot of effort and dedication on the part of the student.
- the best programmes are internationally accredited, and
- both demand the student to defend a thesis or the outcomes of a research project to graduate.

The key differences between the DBA and PhD in business, include:

- the DBA is focused on practical, real-world problems. The PhD in business which focuses on theoretical problems or on theoretical validation and knowledge generation.

- the DBA student is supposed to identify a problem in industry that needs a solution, and to engage with the existing literature in a more applied way. The PhD student is required to identify a gap in the knowledge using a thorough and up-to-date review of the literature.

- the DBA is assessed in terms of whether the research can help address a multidimensional practical problem, while the PhD is judged on the depth and focus of the question.

- the DBA works with business, in other words, there is not an industry-academic divide, while the PhD has little interaction with business.

- the in terms of time commitment: the DBA is done part-time, while working, whereas the PhD is typically conducted full-time.

- target groups: the DBA tends to be pursued by senior professionals, whereas the PhD typically attracts younger graduates.

- admission requirements: DBAs usually require middle management or senior management professional experience while the PhD in business does not.

- professional qualification: for the DBA, an MBA or a Masters in a business management field is typically required, whereas PhDs can typically enter the degree from a good number of specialisations.

- DBAs do not require research experience, whereas it may be required by PhD programmes.

- career orientation: DBAs tend to pursue more senior

management or consulting positions whereas PhDs look to work in academia.

- DBAs are encouraged to work on their doctoral research with guidance from a supervisor, collaboration with business, and if needed, interaction with peers and industry experts. PhDs work on their doctoral research alone with guidance from a supervisor or supervisory panel.

- for DBAs, learning is facilitated both via the university and the real world of practice, whereas for PhDs learning happens entirely through the university.

- the problems identified by DBA studies are student and industry-driven, whereas those of PhDs are driven by prior research.

- in the DBA, the research outcomes apply mostly to the industry where the research took place, whereas the research outcomes of PhDs have a wider academic relevance.

- One issue that still persists between the PhD in business and the DBA is the perception that the PhD is a first-rate degree, benefitting from widespread prestige, while the DBA is considered as second rate (Neumann, 2005). A probable reason for this is the perception that the PhD in business is a top professional degree while the DBA is seen more as a clinical, practitioner or applied doctorate (Kot & Hendel, 2012). Instead, it would be more accurate to see the two degrees as serving different purposes.

Conclusion

Most PhD degrees require high attainment in both scholarship and original research, while professional doctorates emphasize the academic-industry usefulness of the degree and the research carried out. PhD graduates are recognized for their ability to master a narrow, specific field where they are supposed to become the authoritative voice and academic reference in their field of expertise. In the professional doctorate the aspiration is more to use the new skills and knowledge acquired to become a better practitioner. There is also a perception, especially in business, that the DBA better meets demands of high tech and the knowledge economy (Fink, 2006). Given the era in which we live, these are highly strategic considerations.

3

Why Choose the DBA Over a PhD?

Claire Collins[1] and Jane McKenzie, Henley Business School, University of Reading, UK

The DBA is a doctorate of equivalent merit to the PhD, yet it plays a distinct role in the higher education system. Programmes are ideally tailored to build business intellectual capital, because senior leaders and managers completing the programme contribute to both academic knowledge about business and management and at the same time advance business practice. Graduates usually continue applying the sophisticated thinking skills they develop to benefit organisations and society rather than becoming full time academics, although some do move into portfolio careers. This chapter explores in more depth, the reasons why people choose the DBA rather than a PhD and the essential differences between the programmes.

Keywords: Applied research, senior practitioners, rigour and relevance, DBA, PhD.

There are two forms of business and management doctorate on offer in the higher education system. Although they have many commonalities, each makes an essential but distinct contribution to the development of advanced thinking abilities, scientific research, and other areas of knowledge creation. This chapter considers why

---

[1] Author names are displayed alphabetically. An equal contribution to the chapter was made by both authors.

both forms of doctorate are equally important but serve different purposes, and why you would choose to study for a DBA rather than a PhD.

Origins of the DBA

Increasing the value of intellectual capital became a social economic and political concern in the 1990s (Toffler 1990), as Western societies transitioned to become knowledge economies. The origins of the DBA lay in a gap in educational products for senior managers keen to enhance their own intellectual capital by pursuing a doctoral level qualification to both create new knowledge and advance their professional practice (Banerjee and Morley, 2013). In addition, the growing complexity of business and management problems and the intricate challenges of policy makers in increasingly globally connected and technologically advanced societies created a pressing need for research that could be more readily applied to the sort of interdisciplinary settings in which such challenges arose. Universities recognised an opportunity to develop a qualification beyond the generalist Master's level MBA, which could be tailored to the needs of senior executives who wanted rigorous research training, and which would address both the intellectual demands of research and the practical problems being generated.

In fact, the first DBA was offered as early as 1953 by Harvard Business School where it became the 'de facto' doctoral programme for business postgraduates. But at that time, this was unique in the United States, where, as elsewhere, the PhD was acknowledged as the gold standard academic training. By the 1960's a few US universities also began offering DBAs, but often as shorter executive doctorates. It was during the 1990s that the full potential of the professional doctorate was recognised in the UK, Australia, and subsequently Europe. The first UK DBA was offered in 1992 and in Australia the year after. Initially the DBA was generally less well accepted as a rigorous academic training. However, frustration with the difficulties and slowness of complex knowledge transfers from university to business and society, growing academic acceptance of the impact and value of applied research, (Gibbons et al 1994) particularly in social sciences like business and management and careful attention to the quality of research training in the programmes, have since made this an ideal vehicle for developing professional scholarship. Although programme models can differ, the key differentiating principles between a DBA and a PhD are firstly that the DBA gives senior managers an opportunity to develop knowledge that is *both* rigorous *and* relevant to their working environment. Secondly it gives them a solid research training that can be applied in their work setting and is also transferable to other settings such as consultancy and policy-making and thirdly, it is often interdisciplinary research due to the nature of the real-world problems they are tackling.

In this sense, the DBA is aimed at a different type of candidate from the PhD. Those undertaking the classical PhD route, often do so because they intend to pursue a career in academia; they generally research in a single area and use the programme to establish a research identity that they maintain throughout their career. A DBA candidate, however, is more likely to want to use the knowledge produced to further their professional practice, whether that is in business, consultancy, entrepreneurial activity, or work in policy or public sector institutions. Hence, the career trajectory of DBA graduates tends to be more diverse, and they may even progress to keeping a foot in both the academic and practitioner worlds through a portfolio career.

The DBA and the PhD are generally recognised as having equal merit. Yet, it is worth mentioning here, that on occasions, the award does require some explanation to non-experts. Despite the fact that graduates are entitled to adopt the designation 'Dr' the DBA lacks the long history and tradition of the PhD, so for some it does not have the same cachet. It is important to emphasise that both qualifications are equally demanding in terms of the rigour surrounding the process of social scientific research. Accredited institutions comply with the same quality standards for both degrees and examiners evaluate the research against largely the same criteria, with one <u>additional</u> requirement: namely that DBA candidates are asked to demonstrate a contribution to practice. Consequently, the DBA is now well recognised both in academia and higher echelons of government, organisations, and society as an equally rigorous but more relevant doctorate for the professional practice domain. In addition, there are professional bodies, such as AMBA and the Executive DBA Council (EDBAC), whose work includes accreditation of the DBA and who serve to educate the non-expert in the rigour and value of undertaking DBA research. The aim is to build awareness globally that the newer DBA and the longstanding PhD are of equal merit but serve different purposes.

Choosing a DBA

In order to undertake a DBA, senior leaders in organisations generally enter the programme with a Master's degree in a relevant management subject. This has the advantage of having given them some preliminary research training. Most arrive having had many years of experience in their chosen field. Some programmes recognise those years of experience in place of a post graduate degree. This longstanding experience can bring much value to the DBA programme. Having greater and/or wider experience can allow a candidate to see a problem in a wider context and to support other students in similar fields as they progress through their research. On the other hand, a lack of recent formal education can render the experienced candidate somewhat 'rusty' and so the taught elements of a DBA programme are likely be given great attention to help bring those learning skills up to date.

Candidates who have progressed to senior leadership, or high potentials aspiring to that position, are often looking for two complementary returns on their investment; firstly, to differentiate themselves from other managers and give themselves an 'edge' for further promotion, and secondly, to achieve a means of developing competitive advantage for their organisation, so as to achieve greater impact in their industry or to innovate into a new market position.

The principal reasons for choosing a DBA, over a PhD are:

- Being able to demonstrate a contribution to knowledge in business and management *as well as* addressing problems whose solutions advance business practice.

- The opportunity to study while keeping both feet in the business world (part-time status) and maintaining a strong career trajectory.

- As an investment in career and personal development that can differentiate a senior business executive and their organisation.

- To innovate and change direction in their career,

perhaps into consultancy, or even into academia on a part-time basis. This is often the case for senior executives in the mature stages of their career when they want to 'give back' by sharing their knowledge and expertise. They may also act as business mentors or sponsors to younger managers, or as expert speakers sharing domain-specific knowledge and expertise.

- To add rigor to the process of investigating and dealing with complex, multi-disciplinary business problems.

- On occasions, intense curiosity to find an answer to a problem that has perplexed the candidate throughout their business life will prompt retired or financially secure individuals to pursue a DBA simply for personal fulfilment.

The choice to undertake a DBA is, therefore, often guided by the problem being addressed. Practising senior managers will encounter issues which are difficult to solve and may be classed as 'wicked problems' (Rittel & Webber, 1973). As a reflection of the real-world challenges DBA candidates face, their research topics often extend or cross conventional academic disciplinary boundaries. For example, research to understand a particular wicked problem may combine the disciplines of management with psychology, law, sociology, agriculture, manufacturing, or many other domains. The DBA is exactly designed to support research into such complex problems.

It is easy to see how such work can be impactful at a number of levels compared with research that might be conducted as part of a PhD. Often, DBA candidates are working at one or more levels between the individual, team, organisation, or society. Changes to policy, law or regulatory mechanisms are not uncommon outcomes of the thesis and impact at a national or international level is often seen. Some notable examples win industry awards or national recognition for services and improvements developed through their research. Further, since DBA candidates are likely to be either closely associated with the setting in which they collect their data, or well networked with others in their subject area, this can confer an advantage over PhD candidates, when it comes to gaining access to empirical data. However, it is important to emphasise that this more intense connection with a practice setting entails a greater emphasis on methodological rigour, in order that the research process is not compromised by preconceptions, unquestioned assumptions and bias. Consequently, there is a great deal of emphasis placed on critical thinking, transparency in the logic of reasoning and rigorous research training on the DBA programme.

The structure of the DBA programme contains two linked features, which tend to give applicants confidence that studying a doctorate at the same time as holding down a demanding job really is feasible.

- The first is the design of the research training, which tends to be structured to provide concentrated input at recognised points of specific academic need. The workshops punctuate the progressive steps in designing and implementing a research project, usually providing just in time learning at the same time as connecting the parts which are new learning to the whole which is the overarching goal of producing a piece of rigorous research that makes a worthy contribution to knowledge.

- The second is the mutual support provided by a cohort of people of similar maturity and experience.

The advantage of a punctuated rhythm of workshops is that members of a cohort meet regularly to build peer relationships, will be at a similar stage in the development of their thinking, so can have meaningful conversations about what they are learning and critique each other's work in the spirit of development and friendship.

Research training on the DBA

The research training on a DBA programme is both extensive and intensive. There are usually taught elements which examine how to carry out a critical literature review to understand the context of the problem and to focus on research questions which are relevant yet still researchable. Research techniques from both qualitative and quantitative paradigms are taught, so as to develop a fully rounded researcher, capable of carrying out research in any area, or at least to be aware of the principles for using research from either paradigm in their own discovery. Underpinning the choices in any research design is the choice of an appropriate ontology and epistemology[2] so candidates are expected to understand the basics of philosophy for the social sciences, as well as mastering the methodological principles that contribute to the trustworthiness of the research approach taken.

---

[2] Simply put, ontology is concerned with what is and what a researcher recognises as real; epistemology is the study of the different ways to generate knowledge about that reality and assure that the knowledge is scientific and trustworthy. Both ontology, and epistemology are profoundly important for the approach taken to research and the quality of the evidence that supports recommendations and conclusions. They are also part of the technical language of academia, which any doctoral candidate has to become familiar with. Doctoral students are well advised to refer to good quality philosophy and methodology text books recommended throughout their DBA programme.

By undertaking this rigorous research training, DBA candidates are able to engage with existing academic scholarship in a critical way as well as designing their own studies in a way that can have an impact on business and society. The maturity of the candidate - typically the average age of DBA candidates will be early to mid-40s - often generates a strong commitment to their research. DBA students are usually diligent, hard-working, conscientious and can apply their experience to the problem at hand. This enables them to introduce a practitioner view which can influence and enhance the research process and outcomes. The application of rigorous research to their wicked problems allows the researcher to go to deeper levels of understanding of their chosen field and, therefore, develop both superior knowledge and competitive advantage for their organisation, or profession.

As noted above, in undertaking a DBA, mature individuals have often been away from formal education for a while. The process of returning to the world of education often has other profound effects on the individual, over and above the acquisition of technical research skills. Mature candidates will report that they changed as individuals as a result of prolonged periods in a different working world. Most DBA programmes will actively address the personal development aspects of the course and will structure these so that they protect the candidate from unexpected, perhaps unwelcome changes and also create a more positive environment where personal development can be embraced and become a deliberate part of the change process.

Working solo vs working in a cohort

One of the further distinguishing features of DBA programmes is that candidates usually study in cohorts. Whilst the DBA will often share some characteristics of PhD courses in relation to advanced research training for candidates, DBA programmes usually go beyond this by keeping the cohorts together for other elements, such as personal development, presentations, and workshops. They will also often encourage cohort members to build regular communication processes for themselves and build mutual support networks. Cohorts typically set up social media groups using messaging apps to support each other through assessed work and beyond that into their research. Mutual support is particularly important, as between workshops or group sessions, the candidates may be globally dispersed, so cannot, necessarily, enjoy academic support from colleagues, family, or friends. Furthermore, the latter relationships, whilst wanting to support the candidate in a pastoral sense, may not understand the experience of undertaking research and simply cannot 'talk the language' or experience the identity shifts that often accompany the DBA process. In this way, the cohort system in the DBA can be optimised to provide a like-minded network/community of peers that gives support in many forms, academic, pastoral, encouragement to meet key deadlines, or even access to data for the research.

Conclusion

This uniquely designed product in the market for doctoral education is tailored to help those coming from an experienced practitioner base to become industry experts, equipped with more incisive critical thinking and evaluations skills, a network of peers with similar goals and a deeper understanding of the organisational world. This gives them greater potential for innovation, career resilience and the chance to provide a legacy to future generations.

4

Turning the DBA to Your Advantage: Opportunities and Challenges for Self, Organisation and Wider Society

Claire Collins[1] and Jane McKenzie, Henley Business School, University of Reading, UK

Graduating with a DBA is a momentous achievement. Reflecting on their journey, graduates often comment that they underestimated both the commitment and the consequent advantages that ensue. Obviously, they recognise it is a significant investment in time and money, but there are many less obvious demands and consequences associated with personal changes and the development of a scholarly identity. These are important considerations both for the individual and others around them, family, friends, business colleagues, and employers, who are also investing in the candidate. The impact of the research can be realised during the research phase as well as at the end, when findings can be communicated and changes implemented. The benefits of the DBA applied research is that it is often conducted within organisations, not just about them, as with the traditional PhD. Therefore, the payback can be realised, often even before the doctorate

---

[1] Author names are displayed alphabetically. An equal contribution to the chapter was made by both authors.

is awarded. This chapter explores some of the important considerations for anyone thinking about starting a DBA.

Keywords: Impact, development, stakeholders, collateral.

Introduction

In this chapter we consider some distinctive features of the DBA experience that distinguish it from a PhD. We consider both the personal advantage these features can confer and the associated challenges that need to be managed, particularly with respect to those stakeholders who also contribute to what is an investment in personal development and change. We provide examples of where benefits can accrue to the various stakeholder groups surrounding any DBA candidate and show how challenges of integrating the DBA into work and life are managed effectively.

Repaying stakeholder collateral

Although the DBA degree is awarded to an individual, many other stakeholders contribute resources that become part of the investment in what is ideally a holistic development experience for practicing management professionals. Unlike a more traditional PhD, which is often full-time training with a strong theory/discipline focus and a path usually taken by someone aspiring to become an academic, the DBA candidate continues with all their existing responsibilities and adds new ones. This means they will need to satisfy the expectations of a range of non-academic stakeholder groups who become involved in the orbit of their studies. Each stakeholder will have different investments in the candidate's success and expect different returns on that investment.

Obviously, the primary stakeholder is the individual investing in their own future. However, that is not just an investment in time and money, it is also an investment of emotional energy, intense mental focus, and creative effort, which can take its toll on health and relationships. Hence, in addition to the academic support provided by supervisors, tutors, and peers on the programme, their research is also likely to draw support from other stakeholders, such as family and friends, their organisation, colleagues, and mentors. All will have a stake in and contribute to the individual's success. A well-established work-life balance is likely to be further stretched to incorporate study time, and the surrounding network has to adjust accordingly, although they are likely to expect the DBA candidate still to deliver to an acceptable standard on existing commitments. This inevitably means negotiating certain adjustments to priorities in order to accommodate the additional commitment. Clearly careful management of the interests of self and the network of supporters is an important success factor.

Other stakeholders, such as the organisation for whom the candidate works, an industry or professional body, or a government, may deposit time, sponsorship money, a supportive work structure, or access to data into the support 'fund'. In return they will expect to derive some benefit from the outcomes of the DBA research in terms of, for example:

- The direct application of knowledge generated;
- A report to guide internal improvements;

- Innovation of product or process to achieve effectiveness or efficiency;
- A new policy or guidelines to improve applicability or performance; or
- Analysis which allows public policy to be improved.

As this suggests, for these groups, the investment in DBA research can make a difference at various levels. Results may be influential globally, facilitate societal improvement, industry development or advance organisational, team or individual practice. The following examples highlight the range of contributions achieved by some senior practitioners' research as a result of their ongoing engagement with the wider environment: mechanisms for assuring food security; the development and adoption of new algorithms for assessing credit risk. a pricing model for agriculture; understanding the enablers and barriers in the innovation process for firms within a particular industry cluster; the path to developing more complex leadership behaviour within an organisation; or a competency model for IT professionals that the individual could use in their own consultancy.

Stakeholder collateral arises because a government, societal body or organisation has provided access to research data. This incurs a responsibility to give the stakeholder some privileged access to the findings in a format they can use. For example a researcher hosted by a city to study the unintended consequences of technological investment in smart cities, would be obliged to share their research with the local institutions to help improve their future project planning; a study of the effects of technostress on workers following the introduction of mobile technology in one organisation, produced a separately written report and verbal briefing for managers in the organisation; organisations that hosted studies on barriers to promoting women into senior leadership positions, and the key enabling factors to get women into senior leadership roles, would be interested in recommendations to improve their gender balance.

Improved reputation for the individual and/or their employer can be a potentially advantageous payoff from conducting the sort of applied research that is often a feature of the DBA. Employers who support candidates' DBA research demonstrate a commitment to investing in employees and in the future of the business or industry, so boost their reputation as investors in people and in business innovation. The reputational gain may result in competitive advantage and increased market share, and may make them more attractive as an employer, demonstrating organisational commitment to their people. The candidates themselves can gain recognition as a leader in their field. Where the candidate is part of a consultancy firm, or perhaps leads a consultancy in their own right, the collateral of the DBA demonstrates the ability to think critically and to formulate solutions which may be more effective than those of the competition, as well as being a real expert in a particular field.

It is clear then, that the DBA is not just a route for the individual to advance themselves, or to benefit from new knowledge. It can be advantageous to employers, third parties, or a wider group of people including society. The outputs of a DBA have, therefore, potential to be translated into much wider effects and the distance from this practical adoption is usually much shorter than for translating the knowledge acquired as a result of undertaking a PhD.

Stakeholder investments of a more intimate kind (The Wider Stakeholder Group)

Family and friends have a different stake in any DBA investment. They contribute emotional and moral support to the candidate, as well as sacrificing time for socialising and family commitments or events. In accepting the inevitable reduction in social interaction, and an increasing responsibility for managing the daily routines of family life over a period of 4-6 years, the commitment of family and friends is almost as important as that of the candidate themselves. In our experience, some go further and engage with the content of the candidate's research, providing a willing ear when a candidate is stuck, a sense check of written work, valuable proofreading, or some contribution of relevant data. It is often said that individuals doing a DBA change as people, because the programme is designed to be a holistic development experience, rather than just an academic exercise. Often more intimate stakeholders feel that staying involved while a partner or friend complicates the way they think (Geirland 1996), learns to speak a different academic language, and perhaps transforms themselves, is a price worth paying to sustain the closeness of the relationship and provide each other with space for personal growth.

This sharing of commitment may also mean that the inevitable identity transitions which ensue as individuals transform from expert practitioner to apprentice scholar can be navigated more smoothly when regular and transparent communication becomes an accepted part of the support process. Then the changes to the familiar relationship dynamics which do happen either as a result of sacrificing time and money or through the transformative experience of the DBA, have a logic behind them. They are not served up as shocks to a previously continuous family set-up.

Having considered the advantages and challenges implicit in the relationships with various stakeholder groups who provide active support for the DBA candidate, we now turn to the way in which a DBA programme is structured and focused to deliver specific advantages for the individual themselves.

Differentiating content and structure

The structure of the DBA encompasses a number of different features which may not be present in, or are different from those in the PhD. Both involve a rigorous training in the technical aspects of the research process and, like all students of the social sciences, DBA students are required to understand the philosophical underpinnings of the research process. Given the previously noted potential for faster and potentially wider translation, dissemination and impact of results, it is often even more important for DBA students to pay attention to their own worldview and how it relates to that of others. This is helpful when trying to conduct and communicate research effectively, and with awareness of its ethical implications and any potential biases.

The implication of engaging with research philosophy is an area that many senior practitioners find difficult and frustrating; at times it may seem unnecessarily introspective to managers and leaders trained to act. However, it is that process of reflection, questioning assumptions and perspectives, precisely defining terms and carefully justifying reasoning and arguments that provides rigour in scientific methods. Years of writing effective proposals, reports and presentations, using experiential judgements, incomplete and ambiguous information for prompt responses to rapidly moving business conditions tends to develop an ingrained confidence in their own worldview: yet that view remains tacit and unquestioned. The rigours of providing critical academic arguments and evaluating the foundations of objectivity versus subjectivity can then feel excessively frustrating. Making explicit the depths of their critical thinking process can often be very new ground for many DBA candidates. Considerable effort is required to absorb this new way of thinking, and tutors and supervisors may expend considerable effort to present this understanding in a relevant and meaningful way.

Frequently, when a potential DBA candidate presents themselves, coming from their position of senior, or high-potential leader, they have developed a fixed mindset (Dweck, 2006). They are experts in a particular field and believe that research is simply about writing an extended report to confirm their pre-suppositions, which they can present and which demonstrate their expertise. The educational process at the start of the DBA often has to help them break free of this mindset. In its place, thinking that is more open to introspection and challenge is emphasised and encouraged, in order to trigger curiosity and new ways of enquiry into the field of interest. DBA programmes are designed so that this process is integrated into the learning programme and is sensitive to the individual's self-concept, so that their journey is holistic and welcomed.

Developing the individual

All of the training above is designed to develop research competence and capability, and is further enhanced by a deliberate strand of individual development work to encourage this introspection. Candidates who engage with this in a profound way note that they often fundamentally re-evaluate their whole worldview and their identity. Research that we have conducted (McKenzie & Collins, 2020) suggests that the experience can be transformational if the individual is open to it. This complementary strand of DBA learning provides a value-added dimension to the classical doctorate. It not only promotes the critical thinking and analytical skills that all researchers are expected to develop, but the researcher also learns to become significantly more self-reflexive and questioning of the limits and constraints of their own thinking and the ecosystem in which they operate (Kegan 1994, 2009). Over time what we see as supervisors is that this helps to produce more complex thinkers, with the necessary degree of humility about the limits of their own knowledge and their role in creating developmental conditions for others. Making this a distinct and defined element within the DBA programme under the umbrella of personal development is key to such benefits. In some programmes personal development may even be embedded in the assessment protocol for the degree. We would certainly recommend that this is the case.

This personal development orientation in the DBA also needs to accommodate the implications of two important differences in working with these doctoral candidates. Firstly, since the programme is usually part-time, it typically takes longer than a full-time PhD, 4-6 years instead of 3-4 years. Secondly, full-time PhD candidates often start their doctorate immediately after their Master's degree, so tend to be younger. That being the case, DBA candidates are likely to have more complex personal lives e.g., young family, ageing relatives, demanding travel and work schedules and other commitments. This means that supervision interactions happen over a protracted length of time, and the relationship needs to be more sensitive to the nuances of their needs[2]. In addition, the personal development strand of a DBA should be supportive of these conditions and provide a psychologically safe environment (Edmondson, 1999) to allow the individual to explore, accommodate and adjust to the challenges and make changes.

It is wise for programme designers, supervisors, managers and other stakeholders to pay deliberate attention to the process through which this personal change occurs. Educationally some personal change would inevitably happen even without specific programme interventions. However, lack of deliberate attention risks the process being somewhat random or being inadequately supported, with potentially negative consequences for the individual, either in doing their research or, of more concern, in their life and relationships.

We would expect those designing the DBA programme to take an active view of this personal development process. The structure of the programme should include carefully considered interventions which provide guided exercises, reflection and supervision which ensures that the psychologically safe space is achieved and used well. A number of individuals may be involved in this personal

---

[2] For more on the supervisor relationship see chapter 11.

development process including mentors, tutors and, of course, supervisors.

Tutors, specialising in personal development are key to this process being well structured and monitored. The particular interventions chosen can be ordered in such a way as to incrementally take the candidate through a sequence of self-learning, reflection and development activities. Mentors may be in place who have more of a role in a welfare sense than the tutors or supervisors would, and who might be a first port of call should the student encounter identity, work/life, or emotional issues. Finally, supervisors should be well trained to approach their task from a wider standpoint than the generation of a thesis which will pass examination. The work of Lee (2018) amply demonstrates that there are a number of roles and styles that a supervisor can adopt, and some of these roles pay more attention to the pastoral aspects of supervision. Many PhD supervisors also fulfil these roles, but it is even more vital in the DBA where candidates are likely to have more complex lives. The approaches that Lee describes are key tools allowing the supervisor to create a relationship with their student which will generate a rich research outcome. On that note, it might also be pointed out that supervisors, especially those who went straight into a PhD after Master's could well be younger than their student, who is likely to be a senior executive or equivalent. Paying attention to that relationship and to the personal development aspects is an area which requires deliberate development in the supervision body supporting DBA candidates. A complementary advantage for supervisors in taking on DBA candidates is that these senior practitioners often come with a network of connections into industry (and sometimes ready-made datasets) of which the supervisor can become a part.

DBA candidates, therefore, are likely to go through a number of identity transitions in the course of their studies. They join the programme as expert practitioners and, through a quite individual journey, may take on the identity of engaged scholars (Van der Ven, 2007). This journey varies in the number of transition points, the timing of these changes, and in the final outcome, which may see candidates fully embrace a scholarly approach, where others dip in and out of that persona depending on their environment, and yet others remain firmly as practitioners but with enhanced critical researching skills (Collins & McBain, 2018).

Advantages for the individual

The personal and reputational advantages of shifts that occur as a result of these mindset changes confer various advantages for individuals undertaking the programme.

The combination of clear and robust technical learning with deliberately staged personal development interventions can lead to the shaking off of long-held but often unrecognized assumptions. These can open the mind to new opportunities and ways of examining the underlying reasons for business problems and how to research them.

The opportunity presented by the DBA to study in a multi-disciplinary environment enables the use of connections between different theories and disciplines, and the contradictory arguments in relation to a problem, as sources of creative ideas and fresh opportunities. These can be explored with experts in different fields leading to synthesis of ideas and the proposal of new solutions.

As well as the technical skills of conducting research in the social sciences, the DBA candidate will also develop the skills of critical reflection and will build self-awareness which leads to the ability to surface blind spots and identify implicit biases. These critical reflection skills are enhanced by the creation of time to think, which often leads to more profound reflection on leadership practice and uses the generative power of doubt to make better choices. Ultimately, all this may lead to deep personal transformation that can fundamentally change the candidate's view of who they are and what they are capable of.

Structural opportunities

In addition to the reflexive and holistic process of the DBA, there is a structural opportunity which is less likely to be apparent in a PhD programme. In line with the multi-faceted problems that candidates present as their research area, the opportunity of cross-disciplinary work is presented. The real-life challenges that form the essence of DBA research are often a result of 'wicked problems' (Grint, 2005) and, therefore, lend themselves to the integration of two or more management disciplines. The DBA is designed to take advantage of these possibilities and can combine aspects of more than one discipline, or theoretical domain, to create, extend or test theory to be applied to the problem.

Conclusion

This chapter highlights some of the differentiating aspects of DBA study that deliver costs and benefits for a range of stakeholders. Organisations, governments and society can benefit when candidates focus their intellectual endeavours on a relevant business challenge. The candidate can ultimately benefit from career and reputation advancement in their field but perhaps the least obvious, but most beneficial, change can be the changes to self and ways of thinking that DBA programmes are able to generate.

5

Lifelong Learning in an Ageing Society: the DBA as the New MBA

Michelle Mielly and Vassili Joannidès de Lautour, Grenoble Ecole de Management

As working lives last longer, an increasing number of highly-qualified professionals are turning to doctoral studies later in life. This can be explained by many factors, including the rise in educational attainment whereby the Master's is more ubiquitous than ever before, the professionally-active years are extended beyond age sixty, or the increasing number of professionals deciding to pivot to an academic career after years of corporate duty. This suggests that current doctoral education standards are shifting and will continue to do so, and that more organisations will hire experts with professional doctorates. Higher education institutions should design professional doctoral curricula to meet the needs of this population by placing a strong emphasis on both the theoretical and practical implications of their students' output. Designing programmes for societal and organisational impact will ensure that their degree-holders can positively contribute to their given areas of practice, even well into their golden years.

Keywords: Silver economy, DBA, ageing society, professional doctorates, MBA, demographic shifts, lifelong learning.

As working lives last longer, more professionals are seeking doctorates later in life.

To understand major shifts such as the rise in educational attainment later in life, we offer the illustrative example of the United States, whose market-driven educational economy and high educational attainment rates often indicate broader trends before they shift towards the rest of the world. The US National Institutes for Health (NIH) and World Health Organisation's report on Global Health and Ageing[1] currently paints a disquieting picture of current demographic trends in ageing and life expectancy worldwide, where a historically unprecedented surplus in older citizens brings on a host of dilemmas requiring immediate attention. In the US and Europe alike, the proportion of those older than 50 continues to outpace that of those younger than 50 (He *et al,* 2016).

A greying population hitting the books...

With rising percentages of citizens living longer than previous generations, their working lives are longer as well, as one recent UK Study illustrates[2] Educational attainment has concomitantly risen in the US and the UK, as seniors pick up a new diploma--or two--later in life.

According to the 2015 US Census for example, 32% of US residents hold at least a Bachelor's degree, 9% a Master's

---

[1] https://www.nia.nih.gov/sites/default/files/2017-06/global_health_aging.pdf

[2] https://www.ons.gov.uk/peoplepopulationandcommunity/birthsdeathsandmarriages/ageing/articles/livinglongerhowourpopulationischangingandwhyitmatters/2018-08-13

degree, and 2% a Doctorate. Such an increase in people boosting their educational qualifications has resulted in a kind of *"credential one-upmanship"* whereby a Master's degree is turning into the "new Bachelor's" and the Bachelor's degree may be progressively devolving into the equivalent of a high-school diploma[3] Following this logic, doctoral programmes are bound to flourish in the future.

Paradoxically, a number of reports on higher education have revealed a stagnation or even decline in the number of MBA programmes, with several renowned schools discontinuing full-time two-year curricula. The pandemic-induced shift to online provision has entailed the reengineering of many traditionally 'face-to-face' graduate programmes to accommodate for remote teaching and learning, making it even easier to 'study overseas'. For those interested in obtaining an MBA, this has led to a thriving business education sector in other parts of the world, as well as alternatives such as the MIM (Master's in International Management) and Professional Science Master's. The international reference Master's degree on the higher-education market has however been the MBA.

From the golden age to critique: MBA institutionalisation

Since it was first established at Harvard Business School at the turn of the twentieth century, the MBA has played a fundamental role in the rise of Capitalism. Companies needed generalist leaders capable of embracing all dimensions of a business across departments. In Europe,

---

[3]https://www.nytimes.com/2011/07/24/education/edlife/edl-24masters-t.html

INSEAD was launched in 1957 to offer management training to European leaders and ensure a proper allocation of Marshall Plan funding. Since then, the MBA has progressively become a requisite degree in generalist business education for managers.

Its broad diffusion across business and society has led to its institutionalisation and standardisation, with a one-size-fits-all curricular model occasionally criticised for its conformity to mainstream business approaches. Critiques levelled at the MBA can be best understood in the context of extreme market financialisation & privatisation, growth of overseas conglomerates, increased outsourcing, technology transfers abroad, and the predominance of Multinational Corporations (MNCs) at the expense of locally-sourced labour and innovation.

The popularity of the MBA thus began to wane by the mid-2000s, with its overall value called into question by some management educators. With too many MBAs offering recipes to the detriment of managerial intuition, reflection and judgment, some critics began to suggest that this type of curriculum may actually erode soft skills and oversimplify the complexities of good leadership practice.

This could perhaps explain why employers' interest in financing MBAs or hiring MBA graduates has declined over the years. Without necessarily demonstrating greater skill or wisdom, MBA graduates are simply stated more costly hires as the salary promises of MBA-granting institutions have been accompanied with an actual inflation of salary claims. Notwithstanding such critiques, the MBA degree still remains the gold standard worldwide without being the focal endpoint of management education.

This is where our interest in the ageing population comes in: with business environments evolving increasingly rapidly and larger number of professionals attaining MBAs or MScs in Management, a 'pivot' to the next frontier in lifelong learning appears underway. A growing number of large professional services firms has started to seek out experts with doctorates in business, slowly opening the way for a new, post-MBA educational standard.

After the MBA: Doctor who?

With the rise in both attainment rates for Master's degrees and the number of 60+ year-old Americans and Europeans remaining in the workforce, the demand for part-time doctoral programmes for older students is accordingly bound to increase. This trend will in turn put new pressures on universities to design appropriate part-time alternatives to traditional Ph.D. programmes requiring 4 to 6 years of full-time commitment. With the pandemic-induced shift to more blended online delivery modes, the geographic and demographic diversity of student bodies will increase to include non-traditional students, e.g., those with family obligations, those with disabilities, or those from underrepresented geographies or minority groups.

Noticeably, professional doctoral programmes are on the rise in fields such as engineering, psychology, education, medicine and business administration. As the academic directors of a Doctorate of Business Administration (DBA) in Grenoble École de Management (France), we have witnessed first-hand the growing demand from the United States and Europe, with increasing numbers of highly qualified candidates from a range of backgrounds.

The DBA: Chief Wisdom Officer?

In management studies, the pertinence of the doctorate (as a pursuit of wisdom) is often questioned, especially when doctoral graduates are young and often lacking organisational experience. Fieldwork grounds them in the newfound wisdom, although even finding a site for data collection is often a real challenge.

The DBA appears as a response, as it integrates executives hoping to gain distance from the daily grind to capitalise on their organisational experience. Such distance takes the path of a 3-or-4-year deep reflection on a topic relating to their own professional practices. As they progress on their theses and discover a new appetite for writing, many expect to publish their findings. Since 2015, the number of Doctors in Business Administration publishing with their supervisors in academic journals has increased across AMBA-accredited schools. Others have been encouraged to derive a book from the thesis.

One such example can be found in a DBA graduate from Thailand who published a book on the shift of management accountants towards "business partners" derived from her DBA thesis. Becoming a doctor of business administration gave her the necessary self-confidence to submit a proposal to Palgrave Macmillan (Chotiyanon & Joannidès de Lautour, 2018). After the book was published, she was invited to participate in management accounting curricular design and instructor training, developing the field of practice beyond 'typical' accounting work. This case is not isolated and is an exemplar of practitioner and policymaker recognition, which indicates validation by the professional field of the academic credentials gained by the DBA.

Practiced in theory vs praxis

Instead of moving professional doctoral candidates towards topics rooted in practice and leveraging their life experience, academic supervisors and employers – alongside peer-reviewed publications, conferences, and hiring committees – may push them strongly in the direction of theoretical contributions. Doctoral supervisors and educators in professional doctorates seem to remain engaged in the 'social reproduction' of traditionally elite doctoral education (Bourdieu & Passeron, 1990) whereby they unwittingly reproduce the values, practices, and symbolic violence of the education they received. This approach requires revisiting, as older students, armed with years of organisational experience, engage in doctoral study and push their theory-driven supervisors and doctoral gatekeepers to question the wisdom of adhering to such.

Typically, due to its reproductive tendencies, academia tends to indiscriminately channel most doctoral candidates toward the same playing field as PhDs looking for tenure-track positions in the ever-competitive academic job market. In the context of a professional doctorate, such an approach, although second nature for career scholars, should be resisted in favour of more innovative and non-conformist programmes of doctoral study. This is particularly urgent in the face of our many societal 'grand challenges'[4] that will increasingly require a multi-faceted, complex systems problem-solving approach from the academy.

Aimed at making an impact on business or society and grounded in the author's professional and organisational

---

[4] https://pubsonline.informs.org/do/10.1287/orms.2020.05.17/full/

work context, the DBA thesis should conceptualise and generalise a response to a question of practical interest[5]. For example, one of our DBA graduates specialised in backsourcing devised an algorithm allowing him to first estimate which organisational activities should be outsourced or backsourced and secondly to compute the financial implications (Mederos, 2021).

When an increasingly ageing population is seeking higher educational qualification within the contextual trifecta of climate crisis, a global pandemic, and failing democracy, research from practitioners challenging the status quo from within could renew the purpose and reach of the doctorate. In this sense, the 'new' professional doctorate would not be designed to (re)produce professors and academics alone. It would also address societal grand challenges from the field of practice, thrusting them into the hallowed halls of academia and challenging the system.

A Doctorate (in Business Administration) as continuity

As the titles of the two degrees MBA and DBA suggest, the latter is the natural continuity of the former, and most of our DBA students highlight this need to take further what they learned in the MBA. It is not however a mere extension: the DBA is a research curriculum with a dissertation as final output. The DBA dissertation is not in other words an MBA on steroids!

A DBA should enable a dimensional transformation of the student experience: deconstructing, proofing, and testing the recipes learned in the MBA and suggesting new

---

[5]http://theconversation.com/il-faut-plus-de-formations-doctorales-a-orientation-professionnelle-56861

ones. Not all of the new recipes will become best-selling managerial ideas. Today's scholarship is destined to be deconstructed, proofed, tested and called into question by the next generation...

AMBA puts forth the idea that a "DBA places emphasis on the novel application of theory, as well as the potential creation or testing of theory within the context of practice" (Association_of_MBAs, 2016). This is important to highlight, as a number of applicants to DBA programmes believe that they have four years to write an enhanced version of their MBA professional thesis where they tend to assert managerial "truths" not requiring rigorous re-examination. This common misperception is partially grounded in the fact that some higher education institutions perpetuate the ambiguity, as in the case of certain Australian universities offering one-year Doctorates.

Conclusion: The DBA as educational response to ageing overachievers

Although the DBA has existed since it was stablished at Harvard Business School in 1953, its global popularity skyrocketed in the 2000s, as numerous business schools worldwide started offering it. Its popularity has since continued to increase alongside the dual phenomena of MBA institutionalisation (and accompanying critiques, and growth in 'greying' executives in US, Europe, and beyond). The DBA, and other forms of professional doctorates, therefore appear on the horizon as an evolving response to the significant demographic shifts that will require guidance in wisdom acquisition and diffusion well beyond the MBA.

Part 2

The DBA programme

6

DBA Candidate Profiles and Motivations

Vassili Joannidès de Lautour, Grenoble Ecole de Management, Grenoble, France

Who engages in a DBA programme? What encourages someone to engage in a DBA? The answer developed in this chapter is two groups of people. On one hand, the DBA attracts senior executives seeking out professional legitimacy and a career boost, willing to develop and commercialise a concept or make sense of professional practices through hindsight or looking for personal development. On the other, the DBA congregates executives attracted to academia, some transitioning thither whilst others wish to stay and progress therein.

Keywords: Professional legitimacy, industry, sensemaking, academic qualification, academia.

Differences between the DBA and the PhD have been well-documented and highlighted in a variety of outlets and shared in many different fora. However, what remains relatively ill-informed is the profiles of participants. As a result, there may still be some confusion as to why some people would do a DBA rather than a PhD. Reflecting on the 29-year experience of the Grenoble École de Management's delivery of DBA programmes, this chapter answers who are the DBA students; what are their sociological and professional characteristics; and what are some of their motivations. Two groups emerge: senior executives in industry on one hand and others transitioning to academia on the other.

Senior executives

The main population of DBA candidates is comprised of senior executives engaging in part-time doctoral research programmes after 10 to 30 years of work experience. This population reflects four groups of people, each with different motivations and expectations.

Professional legitimacy and a career boost

In certain professional settings, the title of a Doctor of Business Administration grants its holder a special status. A Doctor of Business Administration is perceived as a doctor embedded in and concerned with real-life problems and not just literature reviews. In this capacity as someone educated, wise and knowledgeable, the Doctor of Business Administration has a certain legitimacy to talk publicly. In professional or policy-related discussions, their voices and contributions matter. Often these executives hold positions of responsibility in their organisations where they require a DBA to feel they can contribute and are taken seriously in relation to other professionals in their respective fields. For instance, a programme director at the World Health Organisation decided to engage in a DBA to gain real academic credit, endowing her with sufficient legitimacy to discuss with doctors in medicine, pharmacy, and other researchers. Achieving a DBA appeared as a necessity when work consists of dealing with active researchers in one's chosen field.

Develop and commercialise a concept

A growing number of executives seek to develop new professional activities as consultants. In these cases, the new activity is directly related to the expertise gained throughout their years of experience. Those DBA candidates must demonstrate their professional legitimacy, as their curriculum vitae or LinkedIn profile states. However, they all acknowledge a lack of a *je-ne-sais-quoi* that would make the difference in the market. After discussion, it appears that academic credentials are required in order to justify their new business venture. Notably, candidates falling within this category launch their own consultancy firm because they have a concept they want to sell, and need to ground their own in research. In these cases, they are interested not just in the title of "Doctor of Business Administration" but also in publications associated with or derived from their doctoral thesis. One alumnus was sponsored by his employers (a consultancy firm) to embark on a DBA. In so doing, the employer was expecting academic credentials to serve as evidence of their concept's grounding in research and to reassure their clients. Of the graduate's admission, this perceived need was influenced by the fact that the major consultancy firms do have research units periodically releasing reports with authority in industry. Pursuantly, having a qualified Doctor of Business Administration would allow this smaller consultancy firm to claim equivalent capability of developing a well-grounded concept.

Make sense of professional practices through hindsight

A number of mid-career executives, both male and female, engage in a DBA after their children have left home. As they have more time for themselves, they frequently reflect on their own practices and routines. Some are questioning the meaning of their work or life in general. They have time to deliberate and ask questions; they seek answers. When they join a DBA programme, they unanimously declare that "now is the right time!" For example, a DBA candidate joined the programme in 2020, a few months prior to the start of the COVID-19 pandemic. She was a qualified Doctor of Pharmacology working for a large pharmaceutical company. Over the years, she had progressively transitioned from scientific activities to embracing managerial roles. The main reason for her joining was that, as her children were now independent, she had time to question her managerial practices and the work processes in her industry. Through accomplishing a DBA, she would make sense of her own professional practices and give new purpose to her work.

This motivation to do a DBA is commonly shared by accomplished executives who have already proven their abilities and are well established professionally. It transpires from their motivations for obtaining the DBA that they have an implicit willingness to fill a void in their lives, rejuvenate interest in their work, and find reassurance as to what their role in this world is. The DBA attracts them insofar as it allows them to address all their personal and professional questions at once.

Personal development

Occasionally, executives approaching the later part of their professional lives, engage in a DBA in the same way they would join a personal development programme. The main motivation is the intellectual challenge inherent in the doctoral journey. When commencing a doctorate, they have no expectations other than to reflect upon themselves and grow intellectually, spiritually or both. For some of them, the DBA offers a breather in a professional and personal life where everything has been accomplished. The DBA fills a void and revives the willingness to do something useful.

In 2017, a middle-aged student graduated from the DBA programme she joined because of major changes in the governance of the company where she had been Managing Director for years. Even though she enjoyed her job and was devoted to her employer, she felt that the work routine and the managerialisation of her organisation were hindering her creativity and ability to think. She stated on numerous occasions that the DBA provided her with an opportunity to maintain stamina through intellectual challenges that were compatible with work-related time constraints. Similarly, a seasoned and successful entrepreneur and counsel to policymakers joined the DBA programme in 2018 because he felt that something was lacking in his life. He had experienced wealth and poverty, health and disease, joy and sorrow, but felt the need to spiritually reconnect. He anticipated his thesis to have a significant impact on his life and considered shifting from the role of mentor and coach to that of a coachee and a mentee would help him develop the humility essential for reconnecting spiritually and becoming a better human being.

These two examples are characteristic of mature executives or entrepreneurs viewing the DBA as a way of reconnecting with their inner selves and making sense of their own lives. In some sense, the DBA is not part of any professional plan but rather a spiritual journey.

Professionals transitioning to academia

The second category of people enrolled in a DBA are professionals interested in transitioning to academia. Some of them are executives seeking a career change, whilst others are already working in higher education and seeking further academic credentials. A common motivation is that this doctorate would equip them to share their own experience with others. Through their thesis, they could share their expertise and perspectives with the next generation of decision-makers through teaching. Typically, such executives have completed the first half of their professional lives and could be acknowledged as 'Professionally Qualified' in most business schools where they would be hired to lecture. Many of them, though eligible for this qualification, are concerned that their 'Academically Qualified' colleagues would consider them second-tier instructors. With a DBA, they would overcome this sense of inferiority.

Share experience with younger people

Since 2010, the majority of applicants to the Grenoble École de Management DBA programme in their forties have expressed a desire to share their experience and knowledge with the next generation through part-time teaching. Some engage in a DBA programme on the recommendation of a university where they would like to teach. They are told, "First, do your DBA." Most often, the DBA is their own initiative, since their willingness to teach appears as a calling without a clear idea of the logistics.

Most of those DBA graduates planning on teaching are already working part-time for a business school. Usually, they teach at the Bachelors' and MBA levels, and more rarely in generalist Masters' programmes. Having them teaching at the MBA level is no real surprise, as they can bring into the classroom their professional experience, the theory from their thesis, as well as their professional connections. Teaching at the Bachelors' level, though apparently surprising, is understandable: passion can be shared with the youngest students and inspire them to pursue a similar career.

Motivations are articulated in such a common way by these DBA candidates that no one example would be more eloquent than the rest.

Move towards academia

A small percentage of those mid-career executives willing to teach seeks a permanent career in academia. These are sound professionals believing they have fulfilled their professional obligations and are ready to devote the remainder of their professional lives sharing with others. The calling to teach is far stronger than for those who only want to work part-time at a university. Their motivations indicate that they want to commit themselves fully to education.

For those aspiring full-timers, the academic qualification is much more stringent than for future part-timers. They believe, more than their counterparts, that their professional credentials are insufficient to grant them academic legitimacy and respect from their university peers. They consider the DBA a prerequisite before they even apply for a university position. Their DBA thesis follows academic canons very closely. Since 2010, a growing number of such theses have been paper-based, namely three academic papers of publishable quality. These DBA candidates must demonstrate to their future academic employer and colleagues that they are scholars capable of publishing in highly regarded academic journals.

Interestingly, when these executives apply to a DBA programme, their initial objective is to join a university in a teaching position. As their thesis progresses and publications take shape, about half of them discover an unexpected interest in conducting research. They adjust their goal accordingly, hoping for a full-time academic position involving research.

Stay and progress in academia

With the globalisation of universities, national public authorities and international accrediting bodies require 'Academically Qualified' staff members. Undoubtedly, the first group to be concerned are those academics already working for a university. As university rankings and reputation have become increasingly reliant on research and publications in the past decade, it has become the norm and a pre-requisite for academic staff to hold a doctorate. In this environment, a number of teaching academics are urged to complete doctoral programmes in order to stay on the payroll. As they are already working full-time, like executives in other organisations, they opt for a DBA: such a part-time programme enables them to maintain their professional activity. There are two types of profiles within this demographic.

Firstly, some academics apply on their own initiative to a DBA programme. Generally, their employer facilitates their doctoral journey by making available some time for their curriculum. They can be relieved of certain courses or can concentrate all their teaching over a certain time frame within the year. Others can continue to work part-time temporarily for their current employer. Such DBA applicants are treated on a case-by-case basis. Grenoble École de Management has positioned itself in this niche since its inception, so that approximately 25% of our 500⁺ alumni have come from this situation.

Secondly, a university may establish a policy requiring its faculty to be 'Academically Qualified' and coordinate their application to a DBA programme and doctoral studies with a partner institution. The DBA programme, like individual applications, is chosen for the flexibility it offers candidates. National authorities can encourage or impose this requirement for qualified staff, in which case entire cohorts of candidates are deployed for doctoral research. In this situation, the DBA is financed by the employer. In 2022, some South-East Asian countries are facing this situation and are actively seeking universities with which to partner in Europe in order to academically qualify their staff. This way, the employer contributes to and evaluates their employee's academic progress.

Be a legitimate higher education administrator

Administration and management are a third type of career offered by academia. Although one may not think of this category initially, it is important to note that similar legitimacy issues arise as with teaching and research. In general, these roles do not formally require academic qualification. Candidates in the DBA programme who hold such a position may feel compelled to demonstrate to the academics they manage or with whom they are interacting that they do understand their roles, currents and concerns. This need has evolved as a result of the managerialisation and commercialisation of higher education (Narayan, Northcott, & Parker, 2017; Roberts, 2004; Saravanamuthu & Filling, 2004): *qua* managers or administrators, they often feel suspected of undermining research or teaching. A DBA programme allows them to fill this void and gain those academic credentials they deem necessary in order to be respected by academic colleagues. As for any applicant to a DBA programme, the fact that it is operated on a part-time basis and offers great flexibility attracts them. Here, engaging in a DBA is a strictly individual initiative.

To illustrate one candidate's situation, when presenting a programme or client ambitions, the Associate Dean for executive education of a business school in the Middle East felt some condescension from academic colleagues. Scholars involved in the design and delivery of these programmes would assume that he could not comprehend the importance of grounding teaching in research and at the very least building this research into teaching. By becoming a Doctor of Business Administration, and by demonstrating to them that he had also conducted research and published his work, he could reassure them about the alignment of his suggestions with academic concerns. Similarly, the Student and Career Services manager of a different Middle Eastern university joined the DBA programme for legitimacy purposes. As her intention was to reach a senior position such as Associate Dean for Student Affairs or equivalent, being a doctor was an implicit requirement. She joined the DBA programme on her own initiative, which offered her the flexibility associated with a part-time curriculum.

Conclusion

DBA candidates have understandably different motivations for joining this type of programme. The taxonomy presented here allows for the mapping of the main profiles of applicants (pre-enrolment) and candidates (once enrolled in the programme). One commonality is that they are senior executives seeking change in their lives, careers or both. Another common motivation is the fact that the DBA is a flexible, part-time programme, compatible with maintaining their professional activities. The title of Doctor of Business Administration is significant and important to them because of the symbols attached to it.

7

Different Cultural / Geographical Motivations

Vassili Joannidès de Lautour, Grenoble Ecole de Management, Grenoble, France

Depending on the geographical and cultural setting where they are working, DBA candidates have different motivations for engaging in doctoral studies. In China and the Middle East, the (academic) nobility title attached to the DBA is a driver. In the Americas, the DBA enables expertise recognition of its holders. In French-speaking sub-Saharan countries, the wisdom associated thither grants respectability, whilst in Europe it shows the ability to think out of the box.

Keywords: Social status, expertise recognition, academic recognition, intellectual capacities.

Introduction

Although motivations for pursing a DBA are always personal, and although some profiles of candidates can be established, culture can also matter. Some more or less explicitly given reasons are strongly grounded in culture and geography. Noticeably, the cultural setting where they are working is more determinant than DBA candidates' own cultural background in taking this route. These distinctions approximately correspond to continents: the Middle East and China, but not all of Asia; the Americas; Europe; and lastly, French speaking sub-Saharan African countries.

Acquire an (academic) nobility title in the Middle East and China

The DBA is a doctorate and, in this respect, grants the title of Doctor of Business Administration. The two letters "Dr." attached to the name operate like a nobility title with subsequent social recognition and status. This is especially true in countries where this quasi-aristocratic title is still highly valued, socially significant and well-respected. A substantial number of executives working in these countries seek this social status and hope to obtain it through a DBA programme. This phenomenon is amplified in those countries where the DBA is officially recognised as a doctorate similar to the well-established PhD.

For example, in Middle Eastern countries, being a doctor is a symbol of respectability and can open doors socially. According to some executives working in Saudi Arabia or in the United Arab Emirates, the DBA enables them to advance and be promoted to the highest possible position in their field. In China, notwithstanding the DBA's lack of recognition by academic authorities, there is a similar attraction to the title. Until authorities began tightening control over higher education, it seemed that the DBA was on the verge of official recognition. As a foreign, Western degree, and conferred at a premium price and as an unregulated title, European DBAs attract many applicants explicitly stating that they desire the prestige associated with these two letters "Dr.". They aim to add these to their names in order to gain respect and credibility.

Many European business schools have considered there is a lucrative market in this country and have launched programmes serving as cash cows. Some other institutions, such as Grenoble École de Management, anticipating the toughening of regulations and unwilling to deliver what could be perceived as an earned degree, decided to withdraw from the country. Indeed, business schools are not just selling nobility titles. They are granting them to people who academically deserve it!

Gain expertise recognition in the Americas

In the Americas, DBA candidates express a strong desire for their years of experience and expertise to be recognised. In general, the title itself is not a driver per se for doctoral studies. What matters most is what revolves around it and is associated with the fact of being a Doctor of Business Administration. What matters more than the title in the US and Latin American countries is that the candidate has published either papers in academic journals or books with reputable publishers. In these countries, the DBA is considered a rite of passage, serving as a gateway for publications. These latter are what our candidates are pursuing, because they provide them with actual visibility and credibility. This quest for expertise recognition operates in two realms: in industry on the one hand, and in academia on the other.

Coming from industry, a graduate from the DBA programme has long been working on a book project derived from his thesis, which he wants to serve as "a flagship product" that can position him as an undisputed expert in his field. Others seek to publish in prestigious academic journals such as the *Academy of Management Journal, Harvard Business Review or the Journal of Finance,* all of which are well-known among consultancy firms. The academic visibility associated with these publications contributes to their professional branding; the facts speak for themselves. For example, in November 2021, DBA graduate Michael Gall and his supervisor, published an article derived from his thesis in the prestigious European Journal of Information Systems (Gall & Pigni, 2021).

In the Americas, the Doctorate of Business Administration is recognised as a full doctorate by a number of universities. Such recognition allows the hiring of its holders as fully 'Academically Qualified' staff. Whilst most private universities do recognise the DBA the situation varies from state to state for publicly owned institutions. Not all DBAs are recognised: only those granted by an institution having one of the three international accreditations (AACSB, AMBA, EQUIS/EFMD).

Gain wisdom credentials in French-speaking sub-Saharan countries

Education is one of the most valuable assets people have in Africa, especially in French-speaking sub-Saharan countries, and is therefore highly prized. Degree holders are highly regarded in these countries because education is both scarce and of the utmost quality. This is especially evident in Togo, Ivory Coast, Ghana, Congo, Democratic Republic of Congo and Central African Republic. In these countries, education equates to knowledge and wisdom. The more educated you are, the more knowledgeable and wiser you are considered to be. In traditional tribes, a Doctor is a highly esteemed and learned individual, comparable to a sorcerer (Lutz, 2009).

This social recognition, and the status granted to a doctor are accompanied by significant responsibilities. Great hope is placed in these wise and knowledgeable people: they are entrusted with the community's fate. They can be appointed to the most senior positions in business and government with the expectation of success. In the event of failure, they are deemed deceivers and deserve to be socially deposed. What matters more than just the title, is that a Doctor of Business Administration can achieve great things for the common good.

A clear example of this motivation is the case of Dr. Amanobea Boateng. Following her thesis defence on female entrepreneurship as a means of poverty alleviation, she was invited to give a weekly chronicle on the subject, which was broadcast on Ghana's national radio. These radio chronicles became so popular that she was asked to launch and head a charitable foundation aimed at accompanying women from deprived communities towards successful entrepreneurship.

In 2020 and 2021, two women from Congo and Ivory Coast enrolled in the Grenoble École de Management DBA programme under the purview of further developing female entrepreneurship and micro-finance projects in their home countries. For this, they both acknowledged the importance of being recognised as wise and knowledgeable women upon achieving their DBA. Both praised Amanobea Boateng's work and research and expressed the willingness to follow her example.

Think out of the box in Europe

In European countries, the DBA does not have the same attraction as in other countries, most people associating the doctorate with the PhD. Although some business schools offer DBA programmes, these appear to be relatively small by comparison to those in other parts of the world. This could be explained by the fact that the title "Doctor" is highly regulated in some countries. In Italy, France and Germany, only holders of the national doctorate degree granted by State-owned universities can use the title. In Germany in particular, the title is an official part of the name and its use is thus regulated. Due to these restrictions on using the title, various arrangements have been made where a DBA graduate can be called "Doctor of Business Administration" in English but not "Doctor" in their native language.

Despite these constraints and difficulties in obtaining governmental recognition for the DBA, acknowledgement comes from professions. As the DBA is one degree they highly value, it attracts a number of executives who recognise its merits as a doctorate. European DBA candidates see little difference between a PhD programme, except that it is a flexible, part-time programme. When individuals join a DBA programme, they demonstrate their willingness to think outside the box and develop systemic thinking skills they may not otherwise have. They deem that the qualification as a Doctor of Business Administration will enable them to fruitfully contribute to professional discourse and advance their careers accordingly.

In 2012, a German DBA candidate working as a manager at PWC was expecting his employer to recognise his ability to develop this broad strategic thinking that distinguishes partners. His ambition was to ultimately be offered a partnership. As a Doctor of Business Administration, who has published on accounting matters in academic and policy outlet, this would qualify him as a potential leader. Likewise, in 2019, a young DBA candidate from Luxemburg, who was on KPMG's fast-track talent programme, expected her employer to recognise her capacity to think outside the box. She was ultimately expecting to be offered a partnership in the next few years after the completion of the programme. In contrast to the aforementioned German graduate, she did not deem it necessary to publish in specialised accounting journals but rather in generalist sources to demonstrate her ability to think broadly, systemically and strategically.

Conclusion

Whichever the geographical or cultural context is, the title of Doctor of Business Administration is significant and important because of the symbols attached to it. These differ from one setting to another but always reflect the same reality: wisdom, knowledge expertise and professional respectability.

8

DBA Programme Design

Emma Parry and Nicky Yates, Cranfield School of Management, Cranfield, UK

DBA programmes have the dual aims of equipping participants with the research skills required to carry out rigorous and practically relevant research and support them in their professional development. This chapter aims to summarise the broad range of ways in which current programmes achieve this.

Keywords: Research methods, research skills, training, research proposal, personal and professional development, deliverable, impact.

Introduction

To become "researching professionals" (Bareham et al, 2000), capable of producing research which is both rigorous and relevant, DBA researchers must be able to embed their studies in appropriate extant evidence, determine an appropriate research design and produce outputs which are meaningful for both academics and practitioner audiences alike. DBA programmes, therefore, must not only equip participants with the broad range of research skills required to carry out rigorous and practically relevant research, but support researchers in their professional development and facilitate them to turn their findings into practical, actionable outputs. This chapter discusses how DBA programmes achieve this.

Programme structure

Notwithstanding differences across DBA programmes, this chapter focuses on common elements, while drawing on an example of a programme based in the UK. As DBA programmes are aimed at experienced business professionals who wish to enhance their skills and make an impact in practice, they are generally part-time and range between three and six years in length.

All courses include some element of researcher training, typically in research methods, to support the development of the research itself. In some cases, particularly in the USA, some subject-matter training is also provided. However, the content, extent and structure of research skills and subject-matter training varies, as does the split between this taught part of the programme and the independent research project.

A commonly seen structure for a typical three or four-year DBA is 1+2/3, where research methods training and other relevant courses are taught in a dedicated first (and sometimes into the second) year, whilst the research project itself does not begin until the second or third year. This allows researchers to focus on developing their academic skills and applying this knowledge to their developing research ideas in the University setting. Programmes of this nature may ask applicants for only a vague idea of the research topic or problem that they wish to address in their DBA at application, and often supervisors are not assigned until the end of the research methods training course. A refined proposal will be produced and presented at the end of the research skills training as a basis for transferring the participant to the research part of the programme. In some cases, this will include a change in registration from a Certificate or Master's level course to the DBA.

Another, less common structure, is for research methods training to run alongside the developing research project so that students can apply their skills as they go along. In this case, participants are asked to develop at least a brief proposal, outlining what they wish to investigate in their research prior to joining the programme, are generally assigned a supervisor as part of the application process and begin their research on day one. The research methods training is then delivered alongside the research project to support the development of both the research and researcher.

An example of the latter programme structure is the Cranfield Executive DBA programme, which is designed around a set of seven deliverables (see table 1) which are completed over the course of the DBA study. Each of these seven building blocks has its own discrete purpose and needs to be produced to a schedule. When taken together, these form the basis or a "draft" of the doctoral thesis. These deliverables provide researchers with scalable milestones, helping them move through the programme and enabling academic staff to assess progress as a shared undertaking. Each of these deliverables is formally reviewed, and the participant is not allowed to proceed to the next stage of their DBA until the work is deemed to be of a satisfactory standard. This breaks the work of completing a doctoral thesis down into manageable chunks with realistic deadlines, allowing researchers to remain on track and complete their full degree in the four-year timeframe. At the end of the process, the deliverables constitute a draft of the thesis which then needs synthesis and updating but not complete writing, aiding final completion.

Table 1: The Cranfield DBA Programme Deliverables and timing

Deliverable	Due Date	Supported by	Details
Deliverable I: Problem Formulation	Month 2	Cohort Week 1	To ensure that the candidate has identified an area of research suitable for doctoral study.
Deliverable II: Positioning Study	Month 8	Cohort Weeks 2 & 3	To ensure that the candidate has identified an area of research that is suitable for doctoral study and is positioned within relevant academic literatures.
Deliverable III: Literature Based Project	Month 17	Cohort Weeks 4 & 5	To ensure that the candidate has identified and justified a research question meriting investigation through doctoral study.
Deliverable IV: Research Design	Month 24	Cohort Week 6	To ensure that the candidate has developed the ability to design and plan a piece of empirical research based on their critique of the literature relevant to their research problem.
Deliverable V: Impact Plan	Month 24	Cohort Week 6	To ensure that the candidate demonstrates the actual and potential impact of their research. This is achieved by engaging with practitioner/policy makers throughout the course of the doctorate and by leveraging multiple pathways to impact.
Deliverable VI: Empirical Project	Month 38	Cohort Weeks 7 & 8	To ensure that the candidate has undertaken an empirical project that makes use of a sound research design and makes a contribution to the extant academic literature.
Deliverable VII: Impact Assessment	Month 43	Cohort Weeks 7 & 8	To explicitly examine the potential or actual economic, practical or societal impact of the research.

At Cranfield, DBA participants begin their research on day one of the programme. Residential cohort weeks provide the tools needed to support them at each stage of their research journeys and align with the deliverable schedule. Research skills training is organised so that the correct content is delivered at the appropriate time.

Research skills training

At its most basic, a research skills training programme will include an introduction to business and management research along with introductions to quantitative and qualitative research methods. Many programmes go further including courses or modules on research design and philosophy, literature reviews, research ethics and academic writing. Due to the nature of DBA participants and the objectives of the programmes, many may also include modules on personal and professional development, and on creating both practical and academic impact. As most programmes are aimed at managers with at least five years managerial level work experience, subject-specific knowledge is often a prerequisite of admittance to the programme. In these cases, the focus is purely on providing participants with the skills and knowledge to plan, carry out and write up their research.

The development of a researching professional with a broad range of appropriate skills to carry out high quality research is an important product of a DBA. Therefore, DBA research skills training programmes need to equip individuals to become researching professionals in a broad sense rather than only to deliver their research project. The Vitae Researcher Development Framework

(RDF)[1], can provide a useful basis for the content of such training. This is structured into four domains which capture the knowledge, behaviours and attributes required by professional researchers. It sets out the wide-ranging knowledge, intellectual abilities, techniques and professional standards expected to carry out research, as well as the personal qualities, knowledge and skills to work with others and ensure the wider impact of research:

Domain A. Knowledge and intellectual abilities: The knowledge, intellectual abilities and techniques to do research. This covers the majority of the courses taught in most DBA programmes under the headings of Literature and Theory, Research Methods and Methodology and Subject matter knowledge (covered in a minority of courses).

Domain B. Personal effectiveness: The personal qualities and approach to be an effective researcher. A strong focus on personal and professional development is key to most DBA programmes directly through personal development sessions or through feedback from supervisors and other academics

Domain C. Research governance and organisation: Knowledge of the professional standards and requirements to do research, essential for any research project. All researchers must do ethical research and follow appropriate procedures such as developing data management plans.

Domain D. Engagement, influence and impact: The knowledge and skills to work with others to ensure the wider impact of research. This is particularly relevant to DBA researchers and is explicitly designed into a number

---

[1] Vitae Researcher Development Framework https://www.vitae.ac.uk/RDF

of programmes through sessions not only on writing skills, but how practitioner impact can be developed and assessed.

Impact is a vital part of any DBA research project. It is this practical focus which makes these projects relevant and powerful. DBA participants generally come to programmes with a practical issue or problem that they wish to address in such a way that their research makes a real practical impact in the business or policy world. Ensuring that DBA participants maintain this practical relevance, as they learn more about and relate their problem to academic literature and theory is a significant consideration. Participants need to continually engage with stakeholders and end-users throughout the programme to ensure that the research remains practically relevant and potentially impactful. For example, at Cranfield, two of the programme deliverables relate directly to impact. This formally and explicitly designs this reflection and planning into the programme, forming a required element of the thesis. This is also the case for the Grenoble programme.

Modes of programme delivery

In addition to structure, modes of delivery also vary across programmes. The traditional structure involves the delivery of modules or blocks of teaching (typically a week) on campus at the University where the researcher is registered. This is typically straightforward to manage for the University running the programme, allows participants to achieve space and separation from their busy daily work lives and can be useful in fostering the development of a cohesive cohort of people studying together.

Alternatives to this include digital or hybrid programmes, which have become more common in recent years, with advances in computing technology and enforced changes brought about by the COVID-19 pandemic. These programmes include some modules or workshops that are delivered online (either live or asynchronous) and some face-to-face. In some cases, the pattern is fixed with modules designated as either on campus or online. In other cases, participants can select their preferred mode of engagement. A number of institutions have also developed partnerships for the delivery of their DBA programmes allowing participants to attend courses in different locations, often internationally dispersed. Finally, digital only options are now available, these typically rely on asynchronous delivery supported by live online workshops and supervision.

Although final assessment of all DBA programmes is based on the assessment of a final thesis or portfolio of work and an oral defence (*Viva Voce*), it is common for research methods training modules also to be assessed. This can be via the use of group or individual projects, presentations and written assessments. This is typical for programmes where research methods training is delivered prior to formally commencing the research project and where the programme structure requires credits to be earned towards the final DBA award. In these cases, the successful completion of the research skills programme may result in the award of a formal qualification such as an MSc in Business and Management Research.

Alternatively, and/or additionally student participation in research methods training can be assessed through the production of the research itself. This may be through the development of research and dissertation proposals, project plans or delivery of research seminars. In a few cases, a formal set of deliverables may be set which break the overall thesis down into manageable pieces of work with deadlines which are then independently assessed and which when assembled provide the bones of a doctoral thesis.

Table 2 provides a comparison of the structures and content of the eight DBA programmes that are currently accredited by AMBA. As can be seen, the majority of key features discussed above are seen across these programmes, a reflection of the AMBA principles. All are part time programmes, though the programme duration varies from three to six years, with four years being typical. The majority require a proposal as part of the admissions process. In most cases this is relatively short, the exception to this is the Gordon Institute of Business Science (GIBS) in South Africa, which requires a well-developed proposal and advises applicants who do not have this to consider studying a Master of Philosophy in Evidence-Based Management as an access route. All of the courses provide some research methods training, though this is variable in duration ranging from less than 10 days to the equivalent of several months' worth of training. Most offer this in the first year or two of the programme, and in most cases a more limited number of additional seminars and workshops take place in the final years. The majority of courses focus exclusively on social science-based research methods; however, Bled School of Management in Slovenia and Centrum in Peru offer more general management studies-based courses. Many of the programmes are moving towards hybrid delivery largely for the convenience of the participants. Aston in the UK is the only school to offer a fully online distance learning-based programme and Henley, Cranfield and Centrum offer principally campus-based programmes. Cranfield, Grenoble and Bled have an explicit focus on impact, including courses as part of their programmes and including a thesis chapter on the impact of the research or requiring researchers to prepare a scholarly article appropriate for publishing in a journal for scholarly practitioners. Henley has a focus on personal development and on research culture, with researchers encouraged to get involved with the activities of their research centres. The Business Science Institute in Luxembourg has a particular focus on achieving impact through the publication of books.

Conclusion

DBA programmes allow participants to undertake research projects which see them evolve from executives to researching professionals, enhancing their careers and decision-making skills in the process. To enable this transition, the programmes supporting these researchers need to provide them with the tools to develop, position, design, execute and write up their research projects. This chapter has shown that how programmes do this varies considerably, but a consistent focus on the DBA researcher as an individual and emphasis on carrying out academically grounded and practically useful research unites them all.

Table 2 – Comparison of the Structure of AMBA accredited DBA programmes (all information taken from programme websites)

Institution	Programme duration	Delivery Mode	Research Methods Training Overview
Aston (UK)	4 - 6 years (part-time)	Online only: self-pace asynchronous distance learning, supported by live discussion and supervision.	4 modules completed in year 1. Develop final research proposal and qualifying report to progress to research phase. Two distinct stages.
Henley (UK)	4 - 6 years (part-time)	Face-to-face: each module has a man-datory workshop on Campus in Hen-ley.	Stage 1: 5 compulsory modules. Stage 2: Personal Action Research Project & Doctoral Thesis. Programme designed around 7 deliverables which when completed constitute the basis for a doctoral level thesis.
Cranfield (UK)	4 - 6 years (part-time)	Face-to-face: 9 compulsory cohort weeks on Campus in Cranfield.	Compulsory programme modules covered over the course of the cohort weeks.
Grenoble (France and USA)	3 years (part-time)	Hybrid: primarily online supported by 2 face-to-face weeks. Also delivered in the US.	Two phases. Phase 1: Training in Doctoral Research in Management Science (16 months). Phase 2: Dissertation (20 months).
Business Science Institute (Luxembourg)	3 - 4 years (part-time)	Online or face-to-face in French, En-glish or German. Taught in 10 loca-tions across Europe, Africa, Asia.	Year 1 seminars focus on key methodologies and concepts. Year 2 seminars focus on data collection. Year 3 & 4 seminars focus on writing.
Centrum (Peru)	4 years (part-time)	Face-to-face: 2-week teaching block every 3 months for first 2 years.	Courses delivered in 2-week teaching blocks every 3 months in Years 1 & 2: 6 modules in each year. Years 3 & 4: thesis seminars.
Bled (Slovenia)	4 years	Face-to-face: one week teaching blocks for first two years.	Year 1: literature review, prepare doctoral research proposal and five compulsory courses. Year 2: detailed research model and research protocol and two elective courses. Years 3 & 4: data analysis, focus on research and writ-ing; research seminars and dissertation.
Gordon Institute of Business Science (South Africa)	4 years (part-time)	Blended: mainly online with Festival week on Campus. PhD and DBA programmes delivered together, both aimed at mature learners.	Phase 1 (year 1): preparation and defence of a proposal - attending 5 Orientation Thematic Sessions. Phase 2 (year 2 onward): ethics clearance, data gather-ing and writing up the thesis.

9

Partnership Between the DBA Supervisor and Student: A Special Relationship

Joy Garfield, Aston University, Birmingham, UK.

The relationship between the DBA supervisor and the student is a key factor for the successful completion of the programme. It can be complex, dynamic, and enriching not only for the supervisor and student but also for the university and for the business organisation employing the student. The relationship can also be thought of as special and a partnership of equals that is mutually beneficial and collaborative. Like any special relationship there needs to be mutual trust and respect together with the recognition of individuality, experience and outside pressures that can impact on the research journey.

Keywords: DBA supervisor student relationship, DBA supervision partnership, research supervision, doctoral supervision, professional doctorate supervision.

Introduction

The DBA supervisor student relationship can be thought of as a collaborative and mutually beneficial partnership that is special or distinctive and set apart from other levels of higher education supervision. It is this special relationship that can provide a conducive atmosphere for growth, maturity and flourishing within the professionally based research landscape and the enhancement of collaborative links between the university and the business community.

The DBA supervisor student relationship needs to balance the professional, personal and study requirements throughout the period of the research. Adherence to academic standards, time frame for completion, personal selfcare, and access to resources also need to be kept in good balance (Lee, 2008). Like any special relationship there needs to be mutual trust and respect together with recognition and accommodation of individuality – each student and supervisor having their own unique blend of backgrounds, experiences, and personalities. This sits alongside the empathy and management needed for the challenges that may impact on the DBA journey. Overall, the partnership can provide reciprocal learning and business/academic collaboration amongst other benefits to enrich the experience for all parties.

This chapter discusses the key characteristics of the supervisor student relationship for the DBA and the special nature of that partnership. A case study of DBA supervisor and student voices from Aston University Business School is used as an illustration. The remainder of the chapter is organised as: section 2 provides a background context to the supervisor student relationship and discusses its key characteristics; section 3 focuses on the case study and conclusions are drawn in section 4.

The DBA supervisor student relationship

At the heart of the supervisor student relationship lies the meeting of the juxtaposed professional and academic worlds. The structure of the professional doctorate starts from a real business or management problem and students themselves have several years of senior management experience; both of which set the relationship apart from other types of supervision in higher education. Anderson et al (2015, p.236) note that "supervisors need to be sensitive to the pressures of practice in the shaping and development of the project, and to its possibly erratic progress, both of which may add further challenges for the students". Furthermore, the balancing and juggling of a professional career and family/social commitments with study also come into play and need to be respected, accommodated, and managed.

Although the roles of a supervisor vary depending on the situation, core roles include providing guidance on the research process, policies and procedures and nurturing and guiding the discovery of new ideas. Supervisors can also help with finding a focus and keeping track of progress taking into consideration minimal and maximum completion times.

The management of equals

DBA students themselves tend to be highly focused, motivated, and professionally knowledgeable with a more mature and sometimes more opinionated thought process. Their maturity and practical judgement and knowledge need to be respected in the supervisory relationship. Madichie (2020) describes it as being the management of equals. DBA students tend to have highly developed views relating to their professional experience and some of them have even more relevant practical knowledge than their supervisor (Morley, 2005). This can be a challenge to some supervisors and students. Although the supervisor student relationship can be, as Dinham and Scott (1999) note, wonderfully enriching and productive they also point out that it can be extremely difficult. Overall supervisors and students are both masters and apprentices in this 'special' relationship, which offers huge benefits for all concerned. And like any good relationship trust and mutual respect are key. However, a good relationship does not necessarily mean friendship which could get in the way of criticality.

Case study

This case study focuses on Aston University Business School in the United Kingdom and is used to illustrate key aspects of the supervisor student special relationship. Aston's executive DBA is for business leaders who want to develop their skills in solving complex business problems and produce a comprehensive research project. It is a part-time programme of study/research. DBA candidates are required to have a minimum of five years of senior management experience and the qualification is generally for executives.

This section brings into dialogue the voices of DBA supervisors and students. Research supervisors and students were asked a series of questions about their own experiences of DBA research supervision and the relationship between the supervisor and student. Answers were grouped into key themes.

Supervisor voices

Supervisor role

Supervisors were asked to describe their role as a professional doctoral supervisor. Overall responses highlighted the role of the supervisor as being one of a peer, colleague, mentor, and critical friend.

"The relationship with a DBA student is quite different from my experience with PhD students. The relationship is more like a peer or colleague. DBA students are well organized (usually), focused and pick up things quickly."

"In my view the main role of a supervisor involves academic guidance, personal tutoring, explaining the regulations, and reminding students of the deadline dates, etc."

"I find that supervision changes throughout the duration of the research. In the first year it is more about tutoring and quite directional. In the second year there is support both for data gathering, analysis together with emotional support and keeping on track. And the third year is more about peer-to-peer discussions, reading drafts and deeper conversations."

"Students are used to professionalism, so I need to be very slick and on top of my game as a supervisor."

For DBA supervisors the capacity to adapt to the changing needs of the student through the various stages of the research is a key attribute for a good supervisor student relationship. Within this relationship, it is important not only to provide academic support but also personal/ emotional support and working with the student as a peer/colleague. Research by Neumann (2005, p.178) also recognises different stages of the journey *"some students are very directed, don't need a lot of support, are very competent and confident and get on with it. Other students have different needs and that is a more individual thing".*

Academic ways of working

Supervisors noted that DBA students can find it difficult to detach themselves from being a work professional and work in an academic way. There is a tendency for them to have a solution and want to fit it with the problem rather than going through the process of research to find a solution in a particular way. Therefore, some DBA students can sometimes become defensive towards feedback as they are not so used to being critically challenged.

"Research scoping is difficult, and students often need advice on this."

"Most new students don't have a good idea about the academic side. Masters level isn't necessarily a good preparation for doctoral study. I need to break it to the students very gently."

"There can be many solutions to a particular problem and researchers need to be open to other possibilities."

The taught element at the beginning of the course can provide students with an initial grounding in research and expectations which can be further developed through supervision. When students are aware of this in advance and it is well managed, then this can help in creating, developing, and maintaining a good supervisor student relationship.

Matching supervisors with students

At doctoral level it is normal practice that students are allocated a supervisory team. A good match of supervisors with students can increase completion rates while a mismatch can have a negative impact on the experience. This calls for a thoughtful process when assigning students to supervisors.

"Students need to be matched with supervisors who have the relevant background and knowledge in the subject."

"I didn't think I could match the level of expectation of the student. Fortunately, the other supervisor had a practitioner background and was able to hold helpful technical conversations with the student early on. So, I appreciated working as a supervisory team and was able to provide an academic focus later in discussions."

"I think it is very important to have a credible supervisory team that complements each other from the practical and theoretical angles."

"First impressions matter. The supervisory team needs to be well-aligned in the initial stages to give the DBA student confidence that the financial and time-investment is well-made."

The practicalities of the business environment need to be reflected in the supervision team together with academic experience and knowledge available to the research student. In this way students will be reassured that their professional and personal interests have been taken care of; and that their academic and business interests are adequately combined.

Recognising student differences

No two students are the same as each other. Each has their own backgrounds, experiences, and needs. The supervisors interviewed have highlighted the need to adapt accordingly.

"The differences between the supervisory needs of individual students are greater than those between PhD students and DBA students as groups."

"Every student is different. It is more of a personal relationship than any other work in the university."

"One of my students is studying just for fun. He has already had a successful career in business and academia."

In this case study supervisors recognise that it is helpful to have regular discussions with other colleagues in which supervision experiences are exchanged. During these discussions the needs of the different students can be highlighted, and learning can be used to enhance the experience.

Student voices

Knowledgeable guidance

Students identified that supervision provided them with the stimulation of ideas through debate and discussion, guidance on academic rules and requirements together with being able to talk through any issues and possibilities.

"The knowledge and experience that my supervisors provide of the subject area is invaluable."

"The discussions help me to be more precise in the wording of my research question."

"The guidance my supervisors provide allows me to research the subject area according to my choosing yet within the parameters that they advise."

"Their feedback is with the aim to improve the quality of the research. I can conclude that I am satisfied with my

supervisors, as I am greatly learning from their experience, knowledge, and guidance."

Having a supervision team that is knowledgeable in the subject area and able to provide academic guidance provides a foundation on which students can be nurtured and grow in academic confidence.

A multi-perspective supportive environment

Assigning at least two *supervisors to professional doctoral supervision provides the student with multi-perspective research advice and guidance.*

"My supervisors operate as a team. Meetings are nearly always conducted with my three supervisors present which means more angles to the subject area are covered and with greater impact than would be the case if I was meeting only one or two of them."

"It is a very good experience. It's supportive and encouraging. It is an excellent relationship. We meet every two weeks at their request."

"My supervisors are intelligent, down to earth, and approachable people."

"My relationship with my supervisors is professional. Their supervisory style is providing me with constant structure and support."

Receiving support, feedback and reassurance enables the confidence of the student to be built within the academic field of discipline. It is worth noting the importance students attach to the regularity and consistency of meetings and support.

Recognising the work-life balance

Students recognise the role outside pressures such as work, and family/social commitments can play in the research process. Juggling this alongside part-time study can be very demanding.

"It is difficult to balance having children which has changed my life dramatically. After talking to my supervisor about my situation my supervisor is understanding of my situation and accommodates my personal background as well as my academic needs."

"My supervisors are considerate of my job duties and commitments, nonetheless, they always find a way to maintain a healthy learning environment."

Being listened to and being given the space to be flexible are highly valued and appreciated by students. The above responses make the point about how much those supervisors who allow students more freedom and flexibility contribute to a good work-life balance, hence enhancing the chances for successful completion of the research project. As professionals themselves, students are in a good place to be able to appreciate this kind of support. This area of support is clearly of paramount importance to students.

A research community

Students note the provision of a support system which allow them to address challenges which emerge during the supervision process. Key to this supportive system is the provision of a helpful learning community which brings together DBA students and examples of those who have completed on time or found ways of dealing with difficult situations. Students find these forums helpful in keeping on track with their research in general and with thesis writing, in particular.

"What has worked well has been trying to improve the connection between the DBA student and the department through things like symposiums, colloquiums, courses where I can get to meet other students and feel part of the community."

"I get to meet students who are doing the same course as me and other academics within the field. Discussing my research and other issues has really enhanced my research approach and helped me to feel part of a community."

Enabling students to feel part of a community of scholars, academics and companies, and not feel isolated is really important and needs to be encouraged.

Conclusion

The relationship between DBA supervisors and students can be thought of as a partnership in which students, supervisors, university, and business all benefit. Although more research is needed to establish to what extent each of those involved benefit, it is very clear that when this relationship works well it adds to the richness of the experience for all parties.

The case study in this research also shows that outside pressures in terms of professions and family/social life have a bearing on research progress. The other key factor is the successful matching of students with appropriate supervisors and establishing a culture in which supervisors provide the much needed and appreciated understanding of the different needs of their students.

This chapter makes the argument that it is important that the working relationship between supervisor and student remains a productive one throughout the research period. Factors for successful relationships between DBA supervisors and students include mutual respect of each other's expertise and professionalism, acceptance of critical feedback, and commitments to rules and regulations.

10

Student Support in a DBA Programme

Nicky Yates and Emma Parry, Cranfield School of Management, Cranfield, UK

All doctoral research is difficult. The combination of part time study and the busy lives of most DBA researchers making completing a DBA particularly so. Access to appropriate support is a critical factor in success. This chapter aims to outline the range of support mechanisms available to DBA participants and how they can be accessed.

Keywords: Cohort, support, self, supervisor, family, employer, time.

Introduction

All students benefit from support from academics, administrators, fellow students, friends and family, which allows them to make the most of their time in education from both an academic and personal perspective. The nature of DBA researchers as senior professionals with busy work roles and family lives means that they require more support than other students to ensure that they are successful. This support comes from a range of sources, one of which will be the institution at which they are studying. This chapter explores different avenues of support available to DBA researchers and discusses the best ways of accessing this.

Personal commitment and external support

One of the most important aspects of DBA success is inherent in the researcher themselves, and their personal commitment to their studies. Doctorates of any kind are difficult, both intellectually and emotionally. Completion rates for even full-time programmes are testament to this, with one in five doctoral students in the UK who begin their studies never completing (HEFCE, 2007). For professional or part-time doctorates, such as the DBA completion rates will inevitably be lower. Recent anecdotal evidence suggests that approximately one in three DBA students do not complete their doctorate. All doctoral researchers need to be academically able, highly self-motivated, committed, hard-working and tenacious. These characteristics are even more important for those undertaking a DBA, as they are fitting their studies around the rest of their universally busy lives. For DBA researchers an inherent driving personal motivation to complete their studies is vital. It helps if they can identify a problem or issue which they are genuinely passionate about solving and have a real ambition to make an impact with the research that they are doing. It is this passion to solve the problem and make an impact which we observe as often making more of a difference in seeing participants to the end of the course than those that purely want the qualification or the title.

A part-time doctorate such as a DBA requires a commitment of between 15 and 20 hours a week, in addition to any courses attended at the University or online. This is a significant commitment which is almost impossible to accomplish purely in early mornings, evenings and weekends. Trying to achieve this on top of a 45 - 60 hour a week job every week for four years, is likely to leave the researcher exhausted or unable to make sufficient progress to be allow them to complete their doctorate in a reasonable timeframe. Researchers who actively reflect on this requirement and develop strategies for how they will fit this time into their lives prior to starting the course are far more likely to succeed. Some researchers have the luxury of planning their own diaries and workload or running their own departments and organisations and are able to reduce their working commitments or pass responsibilities to others for the duration of their studies. Others need to seek the support of their organisations and superiors to negotiate ways to carve out the time to complete their studies.

A wider network of personal support is also important. As suggested above, support from employers to potentially fund studies, reduce working hours or responsibilities or permit flexible working modes to allow researchers to allocate significant chunks of time to their studies is crucial. In addition, support and understanding from colleagues who may need to take on additional responsibilities and work around flexible working arrangements or reduced availability for the duration of the research is also important. Away from the office many DBA researchers have family commitments, so support from spouses and family is vital. DBA research is likely to take away from time previously used to perform tasks in the home and family time: if this only becomes apparent once the journey has begun tensions are inevitable. It is therefore essential that this time and space is negotiated at the outset of the doctorate. In addition, the researcher will need emotional support in navigating the ups and downs of their doctoral journey - spouses and families who are involved in the decision to take on the doctorate and fully support it, are much more likely to be able to provide this.

Directly relevant to the practical support needed from family and employers to create time to complete DBA studies, are the working and studying styles of the researcher. DBA researchers are individuals and what works for one researcher may not work for another. The individual needs to work out how they do their best work. Some researchers set aside relatively small periods of time, often two or three hours, early or late in the day, on most days to complete their studies. Others find that this does not give them sufficient space to make progress with their research as they spend all of the time, "catching up", working out what they did last time so that they can make a start - these researchers often find they need to set aside larger chunks of time (maybe a half or full day), less frequently to complete their studies. In other cases, negotiating several days at a time to focus on the doctorate might be preferable. How a researcher chooses to manage their time may also change at different stages of the research, as reading, synthesising, planning, collecting and analysing data and writing are all different activities requiring different skills and levels of concentration and focus.

The supervisor

A DBA is a programme of supervised research. The relationship that a researcher develops with their supervisor is fundamental to their success. This is probably the most important relationship that any doctoral researcher will develop during their research studies and supervisors are a vital source of support. Supervisors will support DBA researchers at every stage of the journey as they transition from business executives to researching professionals. This will involve helping to scope and identify the problem to be addressed in the research, suggesting papers and streams of research to explore, advising on appropriate methodological approaches, assisting in study design and finally giving feedback on drafts of written work, from initial proposals all the way through to the final thesis. Like all relationships the researcher-supervisor relationship must be developed and maintained. At the beginning of the doctorate, it is important to agree boundaries and expectations. The vast majority of supervisory issues and complaints that we encounter as programme directors stem directly from students and supervisors not having aligned expectations and not communicating issues effectively. As often senior managers in organisations, many DBA researchers are used to quick turnarounds from those they work with and work for them. Understanding their position in their supervisors' workload can therefore be a rude awakening! Although supervisors are committed to the supervision of their students, they are one of many competing demands on their time and in times of block teaching or tight project deadlines, the DBA student may not be their top priority. Agreeing reasonable turnaround times for written work and communicating when these will not be possible are important elements of the support the supervisor provides.

Peer support

One of the key features of the majority of, particularly campus based, DBA programmes is the cohort of other students who are moving through the programme at the same time. This comprises a usually relatively small group of like-minded people experiencing the same journey at the same time and thus "walking in each other's shoes". The support that the cohort confers and the impact on achieving success is well established (Stewart, 2015). A researcher will join a cohort at the start of their studies and will go through the programme with them. The support that this group of people give to each other is probably the most important support network that DBA researchers will have during their studies and can provide some of the most profound experiences of the DBA journey. The cohort support each other through the ups and downs of the lived experience of a doctoral journey in a way that supervisors who may have completed their doctorates many years ago and family and friends without doctorates cannot, however much they love and care for the researcher.

Building a coherent and cohesive cohort is an important consideration and one that at Cranfield we take seriously. Our programme is structured around the production of seven discrete deliverables, to a set timetable which when taken together provide the basis for a doctoral thesis. It is also cohort based with each cohort attending Cranfield for nine cohort weeks over their four-year registration, for research methods and other relevant training. Each cohort is assigned a cohort leader, a member of faculty, not generally part of the programme team (though all the members of the current and previous programme teams have been cohort leaders in their time), who is dedicated to the support of the cohort. They are involved in recruiting the students and work with and spend time with the cohort when they are at Cranfield. They are the first port of call, beyond supervisors, if there are any issues and are responsible for liaising with the cohort to tailor the research methods programme to the specific needs of individuals and the cohort. The fit of a candidate to the cohort currently being recruited is a key consideration when interviewing candidates for the programme. Whenever possible the cohort leader will interview all candidates alongside the programme director. Cohorts are given plenty of opportunities during residential weeks to build relationships with each other and the cohort leader (for example during lunches and dinners and in group activities). This mutual support often extends to when they are away from Cranfield through WhatsApp and email groups. For example, one recent cohort have a monthly "Sunday get together" on Zoom where those that are available connect and update each other on their research and their lives, offering each other a further level of support.

Additional sources of support in the institution and beyond

Beyond employers, family, supervisors and the programme team, DBA researchers will have access to other sources of support within the institution. Most DBA programmes have an administration or student support team who invariably have a wealth of knowledge invaluable in helping researchers navigate the processes and procedures of the University. This team can offer advice on a range of matters from research methods timetables, to travel and where to stay, to why a student can't get hold of their supervisor. They are often the first port of call if a researcher has a question or issue.

The wider academic faculty within the University are also valuable sources of support. The DBA programme research skills lectures, seminars and workshops will support DBA researchers to develop the skills that they need to design, carry out and write up their research. Those academics who teach on the research skills training programme will generally be willing to offer advice outside of the class to discuss individual research projects, advising on detailed elements of study design, data collection and analysis. Academics with expertise which is complementary to that of the supervisory team either in subject matter, methodologically or theoretically are invariably willing to discuss DBA projects and answer questions. These academics often form an invaluable resource to advise on subject specific or specialist data analysis techniques. They may also be able to facilitate connections to suitable companies or individuals for data collection, particularly beyond the researcher's and supervisor's own networks. Supervisors will advise on content and, when researchers are interested, work with them to publish their research in academic conferences, journals and books. However, academic writing and preparing work for dissemination is a skill in itself. At Cranfield our research methods training programme includes regular sessions on academic writing but also on specific impact focused communication such as working with the media, using social media, writing for professional publication and developing content for executive education. Supporting students to not only develop their writing skills but also enhance the impact of their research. At Cranfield each student has a progress review team in addition to their supervisors who are responsible for ensuring that the student completes each of the required deliverables to an appropriate standard before the student moves to the next stage. These people have an interest in the researcher's progression and will often bring alternative viewpoints and ideas which help in the development of the research.

Professional services such as the library, careers and IT services offer further support, as do specialist student support services offering advice on matters such as requesting necessary adjustments to the learning environment, dyslexia assessment, access to counselling services (often free to students), or connecting researchers with proof-readers to help with editing and finalising their theses. For example, if you ask many of the DBA researchers at Cranfield who the most important person has been to them in progressing their research, they will mention the dedicated information specialist: her wealth of knowledge and generosity of time and spirit have unlocked many DBA literature reviews. Doctoral alumni also offer an alternative stream of support. DBA and PhD students further on in their research studies and alumni can offer different perspectives and reassurance that it is possible to overcome the challenges and that success at the end is achievable. In fact, a group of Business Science Institute DBA alumni have compiled their advice into a book (Baudet, 2021).

Beyond the home institution, support can be offered by academics working in the same field in other institutions, who may be accessed through the networks of supervisors and the expanding network of the researcher themselves, particularly after attending events and conferences. Finally, support from the wider research community particularly those organisations such as AMBA[1] and the Executive DBA Council (EDBAC)[2] who have a particular interest in DBAs and the British Academy of Management (BAM)[3] with their particular interest in business and management research. This support is usually accessed through attendance at conferences and events, particularly those aimed at DBA or doctoral students, for example the Engaged Management Scholarship Conference[4] which holds a DBA consortium each year.

Conclusion

DBA researchers by their nature as busy professionals require more support than most students to ensure that they complete their studies to the required quality and on time. This support comes from a whole host of sources within the institution and outside. However, the most important driver in successful DBA completion comes from the researcher themselves, their inherent curiosity and drive along with tenacity and willingness to adapt their lives to incorporate their studies are their keys to success. The support that they receive beyond this only makes the process easier.

---

[1] Association of MBAs: https://www.associationofmbas.com/

[2] Executive DBA Council: https://executivedba.org/

[3] British Academy of Management: https://www.bam.ac.uk/ - events page for early career researchers (including DBAs) https://www.bam.ac.uk/events-landing/career-development/early-career.html

[4] Details of past and future Engaged Management Scholarship Conferences: https://executivedba.org/past-and-upcoming-conferences

11

The Supervision Relationship: Working Through Differences in Priorities Between Academic and Management Practice

Claire Collins[1] and Jane McKenzie, Henley Business School, University of Reading, UK

A constructive and developmental relationship between the doctoral supervisor and supervisee is key to success on both PhD and DBA. However, in our experience, the demands of supervision are different when the relationship involves mature and experienced learners with different priorities and reasons for engaging in research compared with the more typical PhD student; contributing to practice and theory, studying and holding down a full time job, working at a distance from the University campus community, and remaining rooted in a familiar practice domain that continues to re-enforce existing habits of mind, are all tensions that alter the dynamics of the supervision relationship. This chapter seeks to help both supervisees and supervisors understand what those tensions mean for an effective relationship. As a DBA candidate, it may be helpful to realise that your supervisor is working hard to adapt well-established and successful routines and practices in order to sustain

---

[1] Author names are displayed alphabetically. An equal contribution to the chapter was made by both authors.

progress and to help you achieve a robust doctorate that still meets the same academic standards as a PhD. The ongoing communication has to accommodate the different priorities for both parties in the supervision partnership.

Keywords: Supervision, experience, practice.

Supervising a DBA thesis

In this chapter we examine the responsibilities of supervisors and the practices involved in supporting a DBA researcher in their quest to achieve an academic qualification at the same time as making a contribution to practice. We suggest that both the supervisor(s) and supervisee at the start have different priorities and perspectives so the relationship will benefit from both parties taking a considered approach to the sources of their differences to ensure that what will be a long-term association (4-6 years) is fruitful. Different world views arise because each party is deeply imbued in the norms and values upholding successful practice in academia and business. Inevitably this results in potentially controversial interactions. Yet the differences can be a productive source of learning on both sides, providing each retains an open mindset (Dweck, 2006) and a desire for mutual understanding. If frustrated by misunderstanding, starved by periods of drought in communication, denuded by lack of meaningful dialogue about all the academic and personal development milestones on the road to 'doctorateness', neither party can achieve their shared concern: to complete the thesis, convince the examiners at viva and graduate as a new member of the academic community. Both parties to the relationship have a responsibility to work with their differences and adapt in order to create a more polished result.

Most issues that occur in DBA supervision relationships arise due to misalignment between supervisee needs and supervisor expectations typically derived from supervising PhDs. It is helpful for an incoming DBA candidate to understand the path to expertise that supervisors take. Successful supervisors will have learned their craft over many years, mostly through hands on experience of supervising younger less experienced PhD students, who tend to start their studies straight after a Masters' degree, without directly experiencing the complexities of business and who are aiming for an academic career. Supervision is a complex multifaceted role. Mature supervisors learn how to wield their skills in a dynamic and versatile manner. Although supervisor training is a feature of many accredited universities, realistically early supervisors might be expected to show less versatility, simply because most supervisor development happens on the job. In line with an apprenticeship model a more experienced first supervisor is paired with an early career second supervisor to develop the complexity of skills required. Every doctorate and every personal journey is unique, so it can take many years to become an expert supervisor.

When misalignment occurs in the supervision relationship, sometimes it is due to practical aspects of engagement between supervisor and supervisee, such as the frequency of interactions, the format and structure of the programme, and awareness of the life challenges mature working manager's experience. This demonstrates the need for the DBA to be more than simply an academic training programme. As discussed in chapter 4, programmes are designed as a holistic process to develop and change the individual beyond their expert practitioner status to become a scholar in their chosen field. As we shall see, that change entails negotiating a path between some apparently contradictory attitudes, beliefs and perspectives on what good looks like in practice. Additional supervisor training to raise awareness of the unique dimensions of DBA supervision when the supervisee is studying under substantially different conditions is a feature of good quality DBA programmes.

Practical aspects of engaging with your supervisor

We are now a long way from the apocryphal 'Oxford' model where a student would meet their supervisor briefly at the beginning of the year to be told to return in three years' time with their thesis fully formed.

The DBA is usually a part-time degree taken over a relatively long period of time, probably 4-6 years, rather than 3-4 years for a full-time doctoral programme. Therefore, supervision meetings may follow a less frequent rhythm and are less likely to be face-to-face, because the supervisee lives and works away from the university. This can make it awkward to engage in difficult conversations and easier for the supervisor to lose track of what is happening in the DBA candidate's world. For the supervisee irregular meetings can mean they feel guilty about lack of progress, and reticent to contact the supervisor. For the supervisor, who does not regularly encounter their supervisee on campus, the consequence is that time passes without knowledge of whether the candidate is progressing or is languishing and needs input. The obvious route through this dilemma is to establish a regular rhythm of writing and meeting and both parties to honour the commitment, even if it feels forced initially.

Peer support is an important adjunct to managing your supervisor. This mutual support is important to calibrate expectations for the supervisee. Studying at a distance, unfortunately means that DBA researchers can get less moral support from peers who may be experiencing similar challenges either in the research, from supervisors or in work-life balance. There is less chance to compare notes, share experiences and work through problems with fellow doctoral students. Although the cohort structure of a DBA compensates to some extent, especially where informal support can be established through messaging groups etc., the distance from a thriving doctoral community adds weight to the importance of supervisor sensitivity to practical and motivational obstacles that may undermine progress for the DBA researcher.

DBA candidates are, by definition, more mature individuals with responsible roles and several years of management experience, so their capacity to work on their research is shaped by their capacity to dedicate time and manage competing demands. Often the immediate and unpredictable pressures of a full-time career can disrupt their plans for progressing their research; health issues and family responsibilities also place an additional stress on planning. They may only get fragmented time slots to study, which are not ideal for complex thinking. Hence progress on particular tasks is unlikely to follow a fixed pattern. The flow of written work may be patchy, punctuated by intense periods of activity and less intense periods. Clearly the supervisor needs to be especially adaptable and creative in finding ways to motivate, engage and sustain progress. Whilst they understand that work and life pressures mean that sometimes research will be at the bottom of the supervisees list, supervisors can only suggest ways to accommodate the various pressures within a broad plan for completion if they are made aware of the reality of the DBA researcher's situation.

Both sides of the supervisor/supervisee partnership have responsibilities in these instances. The supervisor's responsibilities include being sensitive to and aware of the stresses and strains in candidate's context and their level of self-determination. Supervisees have a responsibility to be honest about the problems and challenges they are facing which may impinge on research progress, even when they may feel hesitant about admitting that they are stuck or not coping.

Sources of controversy in the relationship: Different priorities that shape the academic/practice worlds

Some of the more detailed activities involved in the process of DBA supervision include working together to discuss some crucial tensions that arise as a result of contradictory and challenging priorities in the academic world, compared with the more familiar priorities of business and management practice with which the candidate has learned to comply (Table 1).

Each party in the supervisor/supervisee partnership is deeply embedded in the priorities of their immediate context. Contradictions between each column of Table 1 can create tacit tension and profound misunderstandings in the supervision relationship, which can only surface and be addressed in meaningful dialogue. Further, since the DBA candidate usually continues working during their academic training, their practice priorities are constantly being re-enforced. When this re-enforcement is only punctuated by sporadic and infrequent conversations with the supervisor who is deeply imbued in their academic priorities, miscommunication problems arise. The tensions in Table 1 are likely to underpin the sense-making between supervisor and supervisee for a considerable time. Regular dialogue in the relationship is the only place where these differences can be worked through.

Table 1: Contradictory priorities inherent in supervising DBAs (based on Bartunek & Rynes, 2014).

Priorities in the academic world	Priorities in business and management practice
Rigour	Relevance
Logical abstract reasoning in deep and narrow areas	Logic of practice involves action in broad entangled areas of activity
Credible communication builds from evidence to conclusion	Credible communication is short, concise, and focused on answers first
Incentivised and measured on publications and supervisions	Incentivised and measured on business results

We also note that it is the DBA candidate who has signed up to the process of personal development and even identity change during the course of their degree, therefore, supervision needs to accommodate the personal changes of beliefs and values too. From a supervisor's perspective, changing priorities which have become deeply embedded mental dispositions about what good management practice look like, tends to be one of the most difficult parts of the role. In many senses, it boils down to interventions that:

- Change the weight of emphasis from action to critical reflection, and from the value of concrete experience to the value of conceptualisation (Kolb 1976).
- Help the supervisee adequately scope the literature and identify methodological approaches that could partially satisfy their natural desire to solve complex yet too broadly scoped problems that are relevant in practice but difficult to reconcile with narrower methodological and philosophical principles.
- Develop the research knowledge of what is involved in communicating an academic argument effectively and satisfying academic standards.

Clearly, from the perspective of the DBA candidate, the end goal of the relationship is not solely an academic qualification and journal publications. From the supervisee's perspective the supervisor's guidance about the dimensions of rigour may seem pedantic, time consuming, frustratingly abstract and detached from the real-world value of finding a solution to a relevant problem. It may feel contentious for both parties as they try to reconcile their different priorities, but the conflict can be generative of new ways to produce knowledge that can make a real practical difference, as well as advancing academic understanding of the business world. In some cases, the answer is to use methodologies that are actively designed to create change in organisations, in others a phased research design guided by a main research question and some sub-questions may produce interim solutions that could be translated into practical guidance before the thesis is finalised. Alternatively, instead of submitting a monograph thesis, some universities allow the candidate to produce three discrete publishable papers that are integrated via an introduction, a discussion and a conclusion that demonstrates the overall contribution to knowledge.

This final suggestion may also help with another consequence of the conflicting priorities in Table 1. Supervisors who are motivated by publication often complain that DBA candidates produce fewer publications from their research. Supervisors work hard to ensure that the supervisee takes ownership for creating a rigorous contribution to scientific knowledge and they want to see the results influence the wider academic community. Unfortunately, supervisees are often put off from communicating their work in peer reviewed journals because it requires more hard work and brings little reward for them if they have no interest in pursuing an academic career. Admittedly, the publication process can be very time-consuming, and often does not fit naturally into the time schedule of a part-time degree. Once the thesis is complete and the newly qualified doctor returns to their busy practitioner world, extending their academic engagement can seem impractical. University acceptance of a three-paper DBA thesis compared with the standard monograph could align the priorities of supervisor and supervisee and allow both to achieve their goals within the time constraints of the DBA. However, it requires very careful advanced planning in the early stages of the supervision relationship.

Other formats of assessable outputs are also possible in some programmes, such as the production of impact statements alongside a shorter final thesis gives expression to the candidates concern for advancing practice. During the doctorate itself, conference papers, publications in either practitioner journals or, better still, the so called 'bridging journals', which focus on translating academic work into more accessible material for application, are worth considering. Co-authored academic peer reviewed papers may be crafted when the time constraints of degree registration are no-longer present.

For the supervisor, the essence of the DBA is to ensure their supervisee contributes to both theory <u>and</u> practice. Although their principal concern is for the theoretical contribution that is the basic criteria for a doctorate, nevertheless, in business and management, their work is enhanced by a closer connection to practice. Working with DBA researchers who naturally possess an intimate knowledge of problems in practice can be advantageous in developing new research areas. Since supervisees are generally more motivated to make a contribution to practice, the relationship can be developed to produce both/and responses to the tensions that divide the two fields of theory and practice in Table 1. Each party in the relationship may struggle with their contradictory priorities, but provided they can build a strong and trusting supervision relationship based on mutual understanding, it becomes possible to discuss ways to step out of well-trodden paths to a doctoral degree, combine their expertise and creatively push the limits of the often narrow confines of theorising within accepted paradigms.

Pragmatic reactions to supervision

Supervision is a multi-faceted role (Lee, 2011). In principle, there are five recognised supervisory practices. Their development in the supervision relationship is summarised in Table 2.

Table 2: Five elements of a supervisory practice - adapted from Lee 2008 and 2010

Supervisory practice	Functional	Enculturation	Developing critical thinking	Emancipation for personal growth	Relationship development
Focal Activity	Promoting rational progression through tasks	Gatekeeping	Evaluation, challenge	Mentoring, supporting constructivism	Supervising by experience, developing relationship
Knowledge and skills	Directing, project management	Diagnosis of deficiencies, coaching	Argument, critical analysis and questioning	Facilitation, reflection	Emotional Intelligence
Initial learner DEPENDENCE	Needs explanation of stages to be followed and direction	Needs to be shown what to do	Only responds to questions asked	Seeks affirmation of self-worth	Seeks approval
Possible learner response	Obedience, getting organised	Role modelling	Constant inquiry, fight, or flight	Personal growth, reframing	Emotional Intelligence
Gradual move to learner INDEPENDENCE	Can programme own work and competently follow own timetable	Can work independently within academic discipline's epistemological demands	Can reflectively and reflexively critique own work	Can make autonomous decisions about how to be where to go, what to do and where to find information	Demonstrates appropriate reciprocity and has power to withdraw

Each practice has a place at different times in any doctoral journey. However, some may seem unpalatable to DBA supervisees, due to their maturity, expertise and years of successful practice. A supervisor's well-intentioned academic advice may produce a counterproductive reaction. For example, although in the initial stages of the relationship, when there is so much unfamiliar material to absorb, novice DBA researchers naturally feel a degree of dependence on the supervisor, whose *functional* guidance shines a welcomed light on the basic structure and facets of research work. Yet not all DBA researchers arrive with an open mindset (Dweck, 2006); They may resist adapting their strong held beliefs about the problem they want to research. Some find it hard to accept the requirement to narrow down their goals in order to establish a viable research project. The risk is that such individuals become fixed in their position and resist further advice. Certainly, supervisors should discourage blind obedience and senior managers are unlikely to find it a natural behaviour anyway, but the move to independence can be more turbulent on the DBA. Furthermore, if it comes prematurely, and resistance turns to ill-considered action, it can lead to unrealistic expectations and a less than rigorous research design, with potentially disastrous long-term consequences. Certainly, each candidate must find their own voice, but it is vital that the nature of their research question together with critically evaluated justifications derived from the literature drive the research direction.

This tension can be exacerbated when time constraints of work and study exert pressure on the supervisee. People often become frustrated by the volume of reading, the plethora of complex theories and abstract ideas that seem remote from practice, so when a supervisor insists that it is their doctorate, so they must decide independently, and justify their choices based on a comprehensive review of the literature, this can be experienced by the supervisee as neglect or at minimum having unrealistic expectations.

Enculturation to academic norms and standards can often seems tedious and unnecessarily pedantic; the need to define terms precisely and to remain consistent with the principles of a paradigm and a methodology can seem to slow progress towards the intended solution to the identified problem. This delay in action to achieve results can seem quite unnecessary to someone experienced in making choices quickly in the volatile, uncertain complex and ambiguous world of business practice.

Whilst reflection before during and after action and reflexion on the personal biases and filters of the researcher are highly valued academic activities and a crucial part of critical thinking and emancipation, most managers find these practices do not come naturally. They may even resent being constantly challenged. Inevitably, supervisor conversations and written feedback are likely to be peppered with questions, challenges and comments designed to encourage *critical thinking* about the evolving research work. However, it is vital that a doctoral researcher does not become dependent on that as the only way to advance their work. The goal is to develop their own critical thinking and evaluation of their academic choices, as well as to develop comfort with the normal process of peer critique that is part of what gives science its rigour. The supervisor must be able to help the candidate to reach this stage as soon as possible, so that the supervisee becomes able to think independently and the supervisor is able to assess and support more mature work product.

Excess use of critique, on the part of the supervisor, even when framed constructively, can lead, at worst, to flight, but at least can undermine the candidate's confidence and hinder progress. This is one example of why emotional intelligence in the *relationship* becomes important; sensing when something is wrong in the candidate's life, progress, confidence and/or motivation is an important aspect of supervision, as is the facilitation of reflection on both the work and the candidate's own ways of being in order to facilitate personal growth. Clearly, this *emancipatory* role is supported on the DBA by the personal development strand of the programme. However, that in no way removes it from the responsibility of the supervisor. Furthermore, some more mature and experienced supervisees may find it hard to accept younger supervisors attempting to act as mentor and support personal growth. Equally the supervisor in that case may feel inadequate in the role.

An experienced supervisor becomes a successful role model from whom the apprentice researcher can learn the basic principles of research (*functional*), new ways of thinking about knowledge production (*critical thinking*), about one's power and influence in choices made (*emancipation*), the norms that define academic culture both within the institution and within their domain of knowledge, and finally, the paradigmatic orientations that dominate the research culture (*enculturation*). All these contribute to the changing supervision **relationship**. Each supervision relationship comes with its own tensions, and ideally, the supervisor will reflect on every meeting and consider how and when to bring each element into play, using them flexibly in isolation or combination to get different results. However, the key for both parties when these tensions arise is to respect and value each other's differences and engage in a reasoned dialogue to allow the differences to be additive to the research, rather than causing either party to withdraw, or feel inadequate.

Conclusion

Based on these varying issues, supervisors should enter into a DBA supervisory relationship with awareness of competing priorities that permeate the relationship and be versatile in applying a wider selection of skills in order to support the mature and experienced learner throughout their doctoral journey. Equally the supervisee bears a responsibility for being open and honest about the challenges they are facing, keeping an open mindset to guidance, and taking ownership and responsibility for negotiating each key step on their doctoral journey, in a way that takes advantage of but does not become dependent on the academic knowledge and skills of their supervisor.

12

The Gains of Moving Online for a Professional Doctorate

Helena Barnard, Gordon Institute of Business Science, University of Pretoria, South Africa

Busy professionals often struggle to attend on-campus sessions because of time constraints, a challenge that is even bigger if they need to travel from distant locations. For those students, there are real gains to moving online, as it is possible to develop a community of inquiry online. A community of inquiry is characterised by a cognitive, social and teaching presence. The cognitive presence is focused on the individual's process of reflective inquiry; the teaching presence involves the design, facilitation and direction of learning and the social process captures the "community" dimension of learning. This case study of the Gordon Institute of Business Science (GIBS) of the University of Pretoria in South Africa demonstrates how these three presences were enabled and became mutually supportive in an online community.

Keywords: Community of inquiry, hybrid learning, cognitive presence, social presence, teaching presence, Africa.

The gains of moving online for a professional doctorate

Research students in professional doctoral programmes are constrained in terms of the resources they can dedicate to the programme. Even the most committed research student is typically very time-constrained, doing scholarly work in addition to executing high profile duties in their employment. And although they typically have more financial resources than other students, they also seek to invest such resources optimally. For research students who live close to the school, both the time and the financial costs of participating in on-campus events are negligible or at least manageable. But for research students who live further afield, it is harder. For research students from other countries, coming to campus involves travelling, typically via air, and often after the time-consuming process of securing a visa. Thus, the very process of getting to campus is expensive from both a time and a financial perspective.

This chapter focuses on the experience of the Gordon Institute of Business Science (GIBS), the Johannesburg-based business school of the University of Pretoria during and past the COVID-19 pandemic. We believe that our experiences can be useful for any school that is not in a densely populated area. When schools are in dense urban environments, they can focus attracting only local research students. But most programmes gain from being able to attract not only local research students, but also students from a diverse geographical and cultural range. This is especially true for GIBS. There is demand for the school's doctoral programme from across Africa (and beyond), and the school seeks to position itself as an African thought leader. But to attract those students, GIBS has to be fair. A programme cannot offer a rich programme experience for local research students, and a watered-down one for research students who are unable to come to campus on a regular basis.

An initial but sub-optimal solution

Initially, students were offered six annual on-campus weeks. During those weeks, research students were able to present their work in progress, to watch research students defend proposals and completed theses, and to attend masterclasses in, for example, different aspects of research design and methodology. These weeks were also characterised by a number of social events to help the research students strengthen the bonds between them. The research students were urged to attend at least three such campus weeks a year.

Even before the COVID-19 pandemic, there were some concerns about this design. As can be expected, research students who presented (and received feedback on) their work more frequently progressed faster than research students who did not. Unfortunately, also as can be expected, the local research students presented more frequently than the international ones. Moreover, the design required "binge" learning. Even research students who were on campus sometimes did not attend (relevant) sessions, citing intellectual overload. But not only could the design be exhausting, there were also frustratingly long delays – two months at least, and for those who did not attend each time, even longer – between research students identifying a problem and getting appropriate support. Although they had access to their supervisors, research students often preferred to ask questions in a group rather than tie down a supervisor with questions on, for example, a specific statistical technique.

The doctoral programme team at GIBS had identified these concerns, but also received feedback that the support offered by these in-person sessions offered was not only needed, but also appreciated. The team was therefore hesitant to embark on a complete redesign. However, some tweaks were introduced. For example, separate online sessions were introduced for research students who were not able to attend on-campus sessions but who still wanted to present their work in progress. To ensure fairness between research students who lived closer versus research students who lived further away, all of these sessions were voluntary rather than compulsory, although participation was strongly encouraged.

These changes served the school well when the COVID-19 pandemic forced GIBS, like the rest of the world, to move online. Research students were familiar with online platforms and the benefits of sharing their work online. Like everyone else, research students were stressed about the unknowns of the pandemic, but they took comfort from the fact that some of the types of learning they were familiar with were continuing. Somewhat to the surprise of everyone involved, by the end of 2020, GIBS came to the conclusion that the online learning experience had so many gains that it would serve research students best to shift to a primarily online design for its professional doctoral programme.

A community of inquiry online

One of the key models to explain doctoral learning is the "Community of Inquiry" model (Garrison, 2015). Although the model has been used in a range of settings (Garrison, Anderson & Archer, 2010), it was primarily developed to explain online learning. We will now explain the key elements of the Community of Inquiry model, and then highlight how online learning helped GIBS to enhance the research student experience for each of its elements.

The educational experience is at the centre of the model, and is constituted by three presences: The *cognitive*, the *teaching* and the *social* presence. The *cognitive* presence is focused on the process of reflective inquiry of the research student for him or herself. This process typically involves a triggering event or provocation, exploration, integration, and then resolution. The *teaching* presence involves the design, facilitation and direction of learning. For example, it can involve the introduction of a triggering event, or a discussion to guide research students to resolution. The *social* process consists of three main sub-elements: Research students identifying with the community, communicating purposefully in a trusting environment, and developing interpersonal relationships. As GIBS moved its doctoral programme online, changes happened in all three elements. See Figure 1 for a graphic representation of the model.

Figure 1: Community of Inquiry

Community of Inquiry

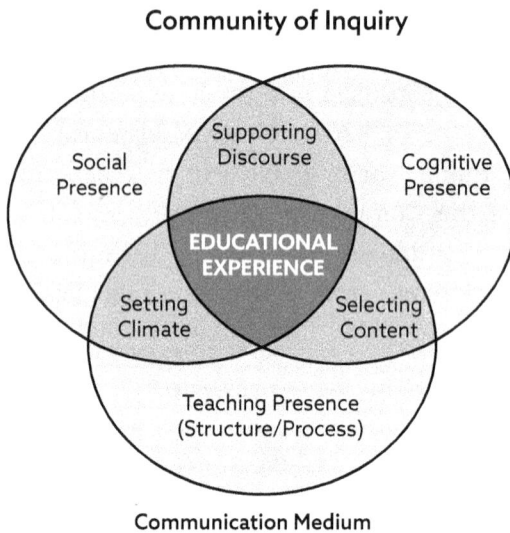

Communication Medium

Source: Garrison, Anderson & Archer (2010)

The cognitive presence

Because research students were curious about each other's worlds, but often not very informed about them, when research students presented their work in progress, their peers were keen to listen to presentations of work on doctoral topics as diverse as gender equity in Nigeria, financial inclusion in Ghana and change initiatives in Kenya. The quite simple clarification-seeking questions of fellow research students ("so how do multinationals get their money out of Zimbabwe?") were often triggering events for learning, forcing research students to articulate assumptions and to make explicit presumed relationships. Research students commented that the ensuing conversations often helped them to increase the rigour of their engagement with the topic.

These sessions proved beneficial for both the advanced and newcomer research students, triggering extensive reflection by both groups. The newcomers were reassured that others had faced and managed to overcome similar challenges. Very often, specific strategies were shared. Moreover, the advanced-stage research students shared not only the lessons learnt, but often also the mistakes they had made. This atmosphere of trust provided useful guidance to the newcomers, but giving help also reminded the advanced-stage research students how much they knew, and how far they had in fact progressed. This supportive discourse was in evidence not only during the class sessions. Sessions also gave rise to more lasting bonds, with research students setting up two WhatsApp groups, one to share academic experiences and advice, and another for social purposes.

The teaching presence

In terms of its teaching presence, going online meant that GIBS could address long-standing concerns about the "binge" design of the programme. Sessions were spaced out better, although, to conserve the energy of research students and faculty alike, the frequency of most of the sessions (e.g., work in progress presentations, ethics guidance and methods masterclasses) did not change. Some sessions were shortened, e.g., from four to two-hour sessions. Only if research student participation directly drove the duration of sessions (especially the work in progress sessions) did the sessions get longer.

Compared with the face-to-face teaching events, the attendance at sessions increased. This was partly to be expected; research students did not need to travel to get to campus. Moreover, if they had a particularly important work obligation, they could excuse themselves from class for the duration of the event, rather than miss the entire day or, if they were international or non-local South Africa research students, the entire week on campus. However, strong attendance was recorded even though this was during the depth of the pandemic and in spite of the fact that many research students admitted struggling to balance increased professional demands, often on top of home-schooling children.

GIBS also decided to introduce a teaching innovation, and to start offering a weekly online writing clinic. Each session lasted 40 minutes, of which about half was facilitation around a structured topic. The other half was an open session to respond to research student queries. As it turned out, many of the subsequent sessions were designed to deal with issues raised by research students in greater depth. This structure allowed the teaching to be quite explicitly directed by the needs of research students. These short but frequent sessions were very well-attended, and research students often asked for help about matters that they previously would not easily admit to needing help with, e.g., finding a balance between over- and under-citation.

The social presence

With engagement shifting almost exclusively online, the relationships between the local and the international research students also became stronger. Before the shift to online learning, relationships were cordial, but the local research students could meet socially outside of campus weeks, while the international research students could not. The stronger relationships across the continents became a resource that strengthened the cognitive presence of all the research students. Although all research students were African, their experiences and thus assumptions were often quite different. For example, many of the research students come from countries that have long been independent. In contrast, South Africa still suffers from the scars of Apartheid. It was a beneficial challenge to all to realise that the South African preoccupation with racial injustice was not a universal one in Africa.

This shift did not simply "happen": GIBS worked hard to strengthen research students' social presence. A monthly online "director's check-in" was introduced for all the registered research students on the programme. Each session started with research students sharing what was on their mind in plenary, often about challenges, whether personal (e.g., related to home schooling) or related to their doctoral studies, e.g., problems with getting ethics clearance. Where research students had achieved milestones, e.g., had completed data gathering, it was celebrated, with many "way to go!" type comments in the chat box. Research students were then broken into random discussion groups with a designated topic that changed each month (e.g., which three scholars, dead or alive, would you want to invite to a fantasy dinner party, or how would you explain your work to a colleague who knew nothing about it?). Attendees often commented that the work of fellow research students was very interesting, and where there were potential synergies, they often shared references.

The mutually enabling relationships between the different presences

As research students and faculty became more comfortable with online engagement, it became clear that the different "presences" – *cognitive, teaching,* and *social* – were mutually enabling. For example, a research student who was in the midst of data gathering, having completed her proposal, but still several months away from writing her actual thesis, said that she attended the writing clinic sessions because they were like an "umbilical cord" that kept her connected to the doctorate in the midst of the many challenges (some but not all COVID-19 related) of her professional and personal life. This suggests that the teaching initiative also served to strengthen the social dimension of the programme.

In another example, during one of the director's check-in sessions it became clear that quite a few research students were struggling to deal with the emotional challenge of coding qualitative data that had been gathered during the depth of the COVID-19 crisis. Certain groups, e.g., entrepreneurs had been especially hard-hit by the crisis. Still feeling quite fragile about their own responses to the pandemic, doctoral research students had to immerse themselves in the data and constantly revisit the views of desperate, struggling entrepreneurs or hospital executives. This insight led to the development of a teaching initiative to offer additional support through these challenges.

The gains of online learning in a data-poor context

A surprising insight had to do with the benefit of the data-poor online context. The GIBS research students are from across Africa, and even within South Africa, connectivity and reliable energy supply cannot be assumed. This meant that bandwidth-heavy strategies had to be avoided. Research students almost never put on their video cameras, and even sound could be challenging. The one reliable channel was via the chat function. However, even when most engagement had to take place through such a media-poor channel, the chat function, the online delivery seemed to be beneficial to doctoral students.

We believe this was due to two factors. First, because of the heavy use of the chat function, going online meant that research students were forced to communicate a lot more in writing. While all research students do better to the extent that they are better writers, a key characteristic of the doctorate is that mastery is communicated through a written piece of work. Thus, the doctoral degree is different from, for example an MBA, where presentations and verbal persuasion are also important components. Faculty members used research student comments on the chat function, and where sessions occurred over a number of days, discussion boards, to facilitate classes. When questions were not clearly phrased, faculty sometimes asked a research student to unmute and explain a comment verbally. But when faculty tried to make sense of a poorly written comment, they could also misunderstand the comment and offer an inappropriate response. Paradoxically, this was beneficial to research students, as it meant that research students could immediately see the dangers of unclear writing.

Second, building on earlier work on psychological safety (Edmondson, 19990), Edmondson and Daley (2020) found that people often uncomfortable with the "spotlight" of a Zoom camera on them (Edmondson & Daley, 2020). In the data-poor African context, no one questioned why a research student did not put on a camera or microphone: It was assumed that connectivity was limited. Unintentionally, this limitation gave research students greater psychological safety. In fact, the extent to which research students were prepared to share challenges and ask even "stupid" questions was much greater than during the face-to-face sessions. Research students also discussed deeply personal topics such as mental health challenges. Compared with the face-to-face sessions, there were fewer cases where research students asked questions to seemingly show off their own knowledge and greater willingness to expose a lack of knowledge. This behaviour took place without cameras – research students would typically put on their camera to greet fellow research students at the beginning of class, and from then would comment without being seen. A few times, a research student would talk and sound emotional, e.g., upset or angry, about something. They consistently muted their microphone after an outburst, continuing from then onwards purely in the chat function.

Conclusion

The primary concern during the first phase of the pandemic was to make sure that teaching quality was not negatively affected. But as the many, and sometimes unexpected benefits of online learning became clearer, the school also realised that it could benefit strategically by offering an online doctoral programme. An emphasis on business and management in Africa had long been important to GIBS, and the online delivery mode made it possible to attract candidates from across the continent. This meant that the school could establish strong relationships with thought leaders from across Africa. The greater diversity of thinking, and the ability to attract high quality candidates from a much bigger pool were both important strategic considerations once GIBS was convinced of the pedagogical benefits of online learning.

But the primary beneficiaries were the research students, who not only were saved the significant time and financial expense of travelling to campus, but who also benefited from more frequent engagement. Moreover, the relative ease and thus frequency of online engagement meant that sessions could be honed in response to their questions and comments. Most of the changes were adjustments to the specific topic areas in regular sessions, e.g., content covered in writing or methods courses. But student needs also informed the introduction of new sessions. For example, sessions on self-care and the notion of liminality helped our research students to make sense of the challenging transition to practitioner-scholars.

Face-to-face learning has not been completely abandoned. There is one on-campus "festival week" per year. The intent is similar to how academic conferences bring together scholars who work with each other remotely for most of the year. There is a flurry of activity before the festival week, as research students try to complete milestones before they present to their peers. For busy professionals, it is hugely energising to deepen their connection with scholarly peers. In short, although the *cognitive* and the *teaching* presences are often best facilitated online, there is value to at least an annual *social* presence on campus.

Part 3

The Impact of the DBA

13

Purpose and Creation of Community in a Professional Doctorate

Helena Barnard and Vivienne Spooner, Gordon Institute of Business Science, University of Pretoria, South Africa

Executives who enter a professional doctorate encounter a strange new world filled with unfamiliar language and practices. In addition, what makes for a successful business practitioner is speed of execution, breadth of knowledge and having answers at hand. In contrast, academia values reflective practices, depth of knowledge and comfort with persistent questioning. While these norms often stand in opposition, becoming familiar and comfortable with academic norms can also be threatening. The scholarly practitioner must learn to straddle two worlds of business and academics, at the same time making sense of the problems encountered in the workplace through both scholarly and practical lenses. We discuss how the development of a scholarly practitioner support community provides a safe space for professional doctoral students to develop conceptual bilingualism. This community offers support to the professional doctoral student because it understands the competing demands of workplace and scholarship.

Keywords: Scholarly practitioner, conceptual bilingualism, evidence-based management, peer support community, theory-practice divide, professional doctorate, dispersed feedback, multi-disciplinarity.

Purpose and creation of community in a professional doctorate

Learning within a community of practice assumes that engagement in the social practice of an enterprise is the primary means of both learning and identity formation. These practices, in and of themselves, form boundary conditions in which the insiders engage with each other idiosyncratically and in relationship, have a nuanced understanding of how the enterprise functions and share a repertoire of meaning as evidenced by having a common understanding of the jargon used. Each of these three dimensions often serve to exclude outsiders (Wenger, 1999).

An executive entering a professional doctorate suddenly becomes exposed to a very unfamiliar set of activities, and often experiences a sense of being an outsider to this particular social practice. Their world of business operates as a separate and quite distinct community from that of the academy, and their identity now becomes that of someone who must connect the practices of these two communities. In this chapter we reflect on the creation of a community of scholarly practitioners to enable the development of a new identity.

The goal for professional doctorates is to link theory and practice. Often practitioners base their business decisions on a range of considerations like their practical expertise, as well as the views of people who might be affected by a decision. But a key component of evidence-based management (Rousseau, 2006) is also a critical assessment of the best available research evidence (Briner, Denyer & Rousseau, 2009). Doing a professional doctorate helps people to become familiar with the research evidence, and comfortable enough with this evidence to critically assess it.

During a professional doctorate, students are expected to attain a level of mastery as researchers, while they remain embedded in practice. Because they work across the theory/practice divide in their separate communities, professionals who undertake doctoral studies become bridges between academia and the world of practice. Students in professional doctoral programmes make sense of the practical problems they face through both a scholarly and a practical lens. To do that, they must learn to engage with existing scholarship. Familiarity with jargon used in business is suddenly replaced by a new repertoire of meaning or, as Corley and Gioia, 2011, p. 11) note, "you people [academics] talk funny". Students' mastery of scholarly norms must happen without them losing sight of their professional goals and without alienating their professional colleagues.

We argue that when students are able to fluently move between the (scholarly) world of evidence and the (practical) world of management, they have achieved a form of "conceptual bilingualism". Thus, they are not simply able to use scholarly insights practically, but they can also challenge scholarship where it does not adequately illuminate practice. We want to suggest that to get to the point where they can fluently communicate their insights both to practitioners and to scholars, a scholarly community of professional doctoral students is central. We highlight first the changed prioritisation that is needed for practitioners to do good scholarly work, then explain how doing the professional doctorate as part of a community can assist in the development of conceptual bilingualism, and finally discuss how the development of a scholarly practitioner community can be supported.

Changed prioritisation needed

Three major shifts must take place in a professional doctorate to allow executives to achieve scholarly success. They need to:

*   shift from a very broad perspective to a much more focused one,
*   move from a preoccupation with answers to an appreciation of questions, and
*   stop valuing speed, and instead to value reflection.

Not only do they have to learn these new ways of approaching these challenges during their studies, but they also have to balance them with continued workplace expectations for a wide, systemic view, clear plans of action and speed of execution. A scholarly community is central in helping executives to develop and practice the three skills: Narrowing their focus of enquiry, focusing on questions rather than answers, and consciously practising patience in the development of ideas.

The traditional model of doing a doctorate is essentially that of serving an apprenticeship in an academic community of practice. Under such a model the individual becomes fully immersed in the academic community, and mastering various research tasks becomes their central focus. Where doctoral students are required to work in exchange for tuition, they are able to deepen their engagement with academia, e.g., as teaching or research assistants. Thus, they need to be absorbed exclusively with the norms of academia in engaging with and succeeding in their work life as developing scholars.

In contrast, professional doctorates often have to make sense of competing norms. The experience can be disorientating. One executive explained that he was used to his board listening to a presentation, asking some tough questions, and then expecting of him to deliver on that presentation. He experienced the iterative feedback process on his doctoral work as that of a weak board that lacked the courage to guide action. Learning to appreciate the value of questions over answers is a necessary skill to enable professional doctorates to straddle their two communities. People who are struggling to find enough time in the day for both work and study, and who may also be under pressure from their professional organisations to meet their study milestones, are confusingly told to stop focusing on speedy execution, and to let ideas develop.

Conceptual bilingualism needed

Professional and academic norms are not only often in opposition, but the new academic norms can also be threatening. Many of the professional doctoral students have achieved considerable career success because they had developed a wide perspective on their world, seeing patterns between, for example, the treatment of employees, socio-economic shifts, technological changes and the work needed in their organisations. They often report feeling that the intellectual work required to sustain such a systemic and integrated view is not recognised, and in fact diminished by requests to narrow the focus of their work. Additionally, the shift from being valued in the workplace as a problem-solver in the face of conflicting perspectives to being questioned about the relevance of their research focus adds to their disorientation. In short, faculty members' comments to hone a research project can be perceived as a threat. And the rigidity that so often accompanies threat responses (Staw, Sandelands & Dutton, 1981) thwarts the learning that is needed. This is where a community of professional doctoral students can play a very useful role.

In such a community, students have the opportunity to talk to the very few people who understand the dual and often competing demands of the workplace and scholarship – other professionals who are also pursuing doctoral studies. In such a community there is a shift in the locus of control from a practitioner-scholar who draws on their deep experience in the workplace to inform decisions, to a scholar-practitioner who is able to enlist and offer support as their scholarship develops.

Development of scholarly practitioner community

At GIBS, we serendipitously started seeing the value of a scholarly practitioner support community when a student set up an online support community for his peers, explaining to faculty that he had created a forum where students could complain about them. He and his fellow students did not want any GIBS representatives joining this support group, but they were comfortable sharing with faculty what was happening in the group. Students needed a forum to make sense of the feedback they were receiving. They wanted to feel free to express their frustration, but did not want to alienate supervisors, which is why they did not want GIBS representatives to have visibility into this forum. Some probing revealed that the primary source of frustration was the novel and sometimes baffling scholarly demands placed on them. This was a safe space to express their confusion without losing face. In this section we discuss the multiple ways in which the peer support group responds to the differing developmental needs of the student.

There is no doubt about the value that this community had for those students. In one case, a student with personal challenges had a discussion with the doctoral programme director about whether or not to deregister from the doctoral degree. Having been guided that deregistration at that point seemed like the best option, the relieved student commented "now I just need to break the news to the WhatsApp group". The response to our enquiry whether her peers would be upset was clear: They will understand, but they will be disappointed.

Over the course of the next few years, as those students were asked about their progress, GIBS also enquired whether the online support community was still active, and what kinds of messages were being communicated. The role of the community broadened as the cohort advanced. Supporting fellow students through tough times remained a key role of the community, including a sense of being with each other during the late night or early morning hours through WhatsApp messages, but there was less bafflement about scholarly norms and expectations. Instead, students tried to help each other with data gathering strategies, for example asking for help in securing access to organisations. As theses were nearing completion, they offered to be first readers for each other's drafts. A very large proportion of this cohort successfully defended their doctoral degrees within about five years.

The success of this initial community was communicated to subsequent students, with the suggestion that they set up similar support networks. Some of the communities were tight-knit and effective, but not all of them were. Because it seemed that the success rate of students was greater when there was an active peer support community, GIBS started thinking how to strengthen peer support communities.

As GIBS tried to understand the purpose of the community, it became evident that faculty could play a greater role in helping students develop conceptual bilingualism by pre-emptively explaining how scholarly norms differed from those used in practice. Faculty could warn students that they were embarking on a process where they would be expected to transition from a broad to a more focused perspective, from answers to questions, and from speedy execution to reflection. The fact that those norms were non-negotiable in an academic context was explained, and students were also reassured that this did not mean that there was anything wrong with the norms that they were using in their professional careers. It had to be explicitly articulated that faculty regarded students as intellectually gifted, professionally successful people who were embarking on a very exacting journey, and that they could be expected to encounter some challenges.

It had long been the norm to invite more advanced students and recent graduates to the orientation sessions of the doctoral programme, with the assumption that newcomers could learn from the experiences of those academically and professionally admired students. But at the outset of the programme students often misunderstood or dismissed the warnings of their more senior peers, with one newcomer writing in the course evaluation that it was unhelpful to try to scare off students at the beginning of the programme. Students likely needed to hear those messages once they started receiving feedback on their overly broad submissions, but by then they often felt so exposed that they did not want to share their "failures" with evidently more successful students.

The doctoral programme at GIBS is designed with a preparatory phase, with the subsequent thesis work having annual proposal, data collection and thesis development milestones. During the preparatory phase, the group forms an identity centred on their intake cohort, but once work on the thesis starts, all students engage as a single multi-year cohort. During the preparatory phase, the focus is on how to conduct research through taught sessions, and in the doctorate the focus is on the conducting of research. In the doctorate there are a few masterclasses on research methods, but the main activity centres on students presenting their work in progress to peers. It is this shift to hearing from doctoral students rather than faculty that led us to a new insight.

The breakthrough happened when students with similar research interests but from different cohorts connected during these shared campus sessions. In animated conversations over lunch, the connection went beyond their shared research interests. Instead, senior students explained how hard but useful it was to receive feedback, and the need to trust the process, even when it did not seem to make sense. They gave examples of professional benefits they had obtained because of their research skills, for example, a news journalist who could improve news coverage by interrogating the process by which opinion polls were conducted. Her ability to critically assess the evidence before her allowed her to bridge theory/practice. When the more senior students were thanked for sharing their advice with their less advanced peers, they explained that responding to the questions of the students who were following in their footsteps was motivating for them. Being able to answer such questions reminded them that although they had not yet completed their doctoral studies, they had already learnt a lot.

Given the evidence that the more advanced students did not experience supporting newcomers as an imposition, GIBS decided that there may be value in introducing a programme-wide support community. This was suggested to students during a plenary session, and an individual volunteered to take the lead on setting up a programme-wide online support group. In the time that was provided to students to ask questions about their anticipated involvement, and to provide their contact details, rules of engagement emerged. These rules were essentially that any social purpose (e.g., sharing jokes) would be limited to cohort-specific groups, and that the plenary group was only for asking for help or encouragement. The lead asked his peers to be generous in responding to such requests.

For the professional doctoral student two forms of support groups have emerged. The public support group has become well-established through frequent and on-going peer-presentation sessions that are facilitated by faculty members. Students present their work, receive feedback from their peers and from the faculty member present. Facilitated peer presentations allow the student to engage with the process of becoming more focused and reflective, as well as developing an appreciation of questions over answers, as was noted earlier.

In these sessions, the competing norms of academic and organisations begin to become normalised through dispersed feedback. In discussions with students about what, if anything, is to be gained from these sessions many benefits and a few disadvantages were identified.

The main benefits include being able to make progress on one's own research through hearing about different theories, methodologies or caveats. Additionally, they gain further research input to their evidence-based management practice because the presentations are multi-disciplinary and there are transferable findings into good business practice and management principles from the literature. Presenters have commented that they could often pinpoint where their explanations lacked clarity, argument or merit simply by looking at the bafflement in the faces of their peers. There is also the advantage of being able to put into practice the skill of narrowing down to a central point they want to make.

Disadvantages that were identified included that there was not always an optimal number of peers and from across the various phases in the audience. Especially for students further along with their dissertation, useful feedback tended to come from the much smaller number of participants at the same or later stage of their doctorate.

However, overwhelmingly students report how the community offers support, encouragement and affirmation. For the newcomers into the doctorate there is amazement at the generosity of support offered by their peers, particularly from those who have been in the doctorate for longer than them. Faculty still does not have visibility into any of the online support groups, nor into other invisible-to-faculty forms of support. In a throwaway line following a presentation, one of the students revealed that when submitting final drafts of work to his supervisor, he blind copies some trusted peers on the email. The group of peers explained that they were often too emotionally vested in their work to properly process the feedback. Their peers were able to read the feedback and to guide them through what was said.

New students onto the professional doctoral programme still express confusion about the acquisition of a different and often competing set of norms to those governing their professional lives. But the way in which they discuss their uncertainty in sessions has changed. They now discuss it as the kind of response that can be expected of people at the beginning of the doctoral journey. To preface a response with a phrase like "I guess I am still too much of a practitioner, but..." has become common. At the same time, more advanced students enjoy sharing the ways in which their research insights have proven useful at work, for example by sharing how a colleague expressed admiration for how clear and systematic their writing has become.

What we have seen is that the peer community bolsters the support offered by faculty and supervisors. The community of peers complements and often supersedes, in a psychologically safe place, the work of the formal support system. Making sense of feedback and plucking up the courage to submit work happens in this support group before the student feels emotionally equipped to take their next steps.

Conclusion

GIBS expected benefits for professionals who are new to scholarship and who need reassurance that they can navigate the new academic norms. It did not expect that the more experienced students would explain the value of doctoral studies to those students by giving examples of how research insights enriched their professional lives. Additionally, during open evenings where the programme is explained to potential applicants, we have asked other doctoral students to meet applicants in small groups. In these closed sessions, a consistent message that emerges is the power of the peer support community.

As students from across the different cohorts participate in supporting peers, they draw on both their academic and their professional selves. In the process, they both develop conceptual bilingualism, and demonstrate evidence-based management.

14

Professional Development and Impact

Chris Owen, Aston University, Birmingham, UK.

DBA research will deliver impact to organisations, to the practice of management and to the individual who undertakes the qualification. In this chapter, by means of five short case studies of graduates of the Aston Business School DBA Programme, UK, the nature of this impact is explored. The case studies show that this impact may include development of deep expertise and thought leadership, personal transformational learning and the launch of new organisational forms.

Keywords: Impact, transformational learning, professional development.

Introduction

There are many varied reasons for embarking on a DBA (Simpson & Sommer, 2016). For some, it is the opportunity to research an area of interest in depth, or to wrestle with a complex organisational problem. For others, it may be a long held personal ambition to achieve the highest level academic qualification. For many it may be the desirability of the Dr. title before the name. Whatever the motivation, there will be an expectation on the part of the individual student that the DBA will lead to some kind of impact, whether that be on their own organisation, their industry or themselves as professionals. In this chapter, we will explore the nature of this impact and using five case studies from DBA graduates from a UK programme, give some examples of what impact means, both for organisations, the individuals themselves, and the wider practice of management.

Impact on the individual - the DBA as transformative learning

The DBA is a transformative experience for the person pursuing the qualification. Many DBAs candidates are returning to academia and their studies at a later stage in their lives and careers. Receiving training in research methods and the rigorous approach that academics take to their research can result in a dramatic shift in the mindset and thinking of DBA students. The DBA experience occurs at an individual and organisational level, and can better be understood as a process of change that is unique to each individual and context (Creaton & Anderson, 2021). The transformation may be understood as the student becoming scholarly management practitioners, more reflexive of their practice and reflecting in action (Rigg, Ellwood, & Anderson, 2021; Schön, 1983). The DBA is more than a form of training:

"...far from being an advanced form of professional training for senior managers, the DBA should be seen as a radically diverse form of education that promotes action learning and critical reflection on professional practice." (Simpson & Sommer, 2016, p.589)

Case study examples

The following case studies are the reflections of five graduates of a UK DBA programme on the experience of completing a DBA. The cases are all very different, both in terms of the motivation of the individuals concerned, and their experience of doing the qualification.

The Olderpreneur

"At the age of 60, I found myself running a business again, this time with my daughter. I had founded a business providing translation and interpreting services to industry in my 30s, sold it to a US-owned company, but then after 6 years had the opportunity to buy the business back. Buying back the business was definitely an unplanned decision, but the opportunity of working with my daughter was too great a pull. As we set about restoring the fortunes of the company, I quickly began to realise, as an "older" entrepreneur, I was facing very different problems to those I faced when setting up my business several decades previously. I suspected also that the experience of setting up in business in later life was very different for men than for women. A chance conversation with one of the teaching staff at the Business School, led me to apply to the DBA programme to research this topic.

I learnt very quickly that I needed to leave my ego behind. I realised that as a doctoral student I was no different in the eyes of the university to my much younger peers. Nevertheless, it was liberating to leave my past behind and just embrace being a student again, to learn from my supervisors, as well as from the much younger students around me. Sometimes, it was a painful process. My brain was certainly not primed to work in a research environment. I learned to listen to my supervisors and my fellow students. At times I felt really uncomfortable and utterly out of my depth. For example, at academic conferences, despite how young I felt, initial impressions tended to be based on how old I looked, and I was often mistaken for an experienced academic! I could not help feeling that behind this reaction was an unspoken enquiry: "So why are you a student at your age?"

This is certainly a question I've asked myself. I fitted my studies in around my life, typically squeezing in my doctoral work during evenings and weekends, but trying to segregate family, work and DBA time was often difficult. I did also notice that older doctoral candidates were under-represented in the teaching and lecturing undertaken by postgraduate students.

For me, undertaking this research was one of the best decisions I have ever made. It fulfilled my desire for intellectual stimulation and challenged me; it was a transformative time of my life.

The Executive Coach

"As the Founder of The Trusted Executive Foundation, my team and I help board leaders across all sectors adapt to the 'new normal' of trust-based leadership using the unique models and tools from my books, 'The Trusted Executive' and 'Challenging Coaching'. The Foundation is a not for profit with a ten-year social justice mission to gift over £1m to UK-based Christian-led charities that are inclusive at the point of need.

'The Trusted Executive' combines my prize-winning research to create the Nine Habits of Trust, together with the learnings from my successes (and failures!) as a former FTSE 100 international managing director and entrepreneur. In 2017, the book was shortlisted as the Chartered Management Institute book of the year.

'Challenging Coaching', co-authored with Ian Day, is one of the UK's best-selling leadership books and features the FACTS coaching model. It was inspired by my executive coaching work with over 130 CEOs from 22 different countries, as well as the leaders of gold-medal winning Team GB Olympic squads, premiership football clubs and England cricket.

I deliver keynote speaker sessions on the Nine Habits of Trust and support a small number of pioneering CEOs as an executive coach. Our team can drive specific business impact via 'Journey of Trust' leadership programmes and Trusted Executive Fellowship Boards, which bring together like-minded, values-led CEOs and entrepreneurs for shared learning and inspiration.

My work has featured in Forbes, BBC News, HuffPost, the FT and The Sunday Times."

The Business Owner

"The DBA process really pushes boundaries, taking you outside your comfort zone and creating space to expand your capacity for studying complex issues. The contribution of my research findings will help SMEs to accelerate their adoption of Advanced Services. Crucially, this can increase productivity, whilst providing environmental and societal benefits. The practical application frameworks developed

during my research programme have already been applied by my company, with immediate impact.

At the start of the research programme in 2018, 25% of the company's annual revenue was derived from base and intermediate services, with the rest coming from product sales. The company needed to find new ways of developing competitive advantage, enhancing productivity, and building resilience. The choice was to go beyond operational effectiveness by transitioning towards advanced services where value is captured during use of their products. During 2020, the first advanced service was successfully piloted and is now being replicated for scale. The latest quarterly figures reveal that for the first time in the company's 24-year history, 50% of revenue was generated from services. This has significantly increased productivity and is building resilience, whilst also making a positive contribution to environmental impact."

The Senior Procurement Director

"I embarked on the programme in order to test myself – to test whether I really did know my subject and to provide a degree of credibility that has been independently verified and was something that I could use to differentiate myself – Oh yes, I also quite fancied being called by the title "Doctor".

The initial phases of the DBA provided the grounding in the academic process that I was missing. I had an MBA, although that was 10 years ago, in addition, the DBA was research-based which meant going back to the first principles with regard to the scientific method in order to ensure that there was sufficient rigour. I found this phase very useful and it helped me to bridge the gap between my experience and the expectations of the DBA. It was at this stage that I realised I really did not know my subject well enough and the end result was that I had to revisit and question everything that I thought I knew which was a necessary (but humbling) experience.

On the back of my DBA experience, I found that I was one of a small but growing population of boundary spanning individuals that has a foot in both the world of academia and the world of the practitioner – some people call us "pracademics".

I saw clearly the academic world would benefit from having a higher degree of practitioner input. I also saw that there was a lot of practitioners who would really benefit from some independent research in order to help improve their profession. This then became a catalyst for setting up The Procurement Doctor – an organisation that is designed to make academic research more accessible to practitioners.

The overall impact of the DBA for me was initially quite subtle but actually proved to be quite profound. It has opened up new and exciting avenues and has provided me with the credibility and the "license" to develop as a thought leader within my profession. As mentioned earlier, the initial effect was subtle in that it changed the way that I thought and operated. In some respects, to an outsider, it made me less "marketable" in my previous profession, as the Dr title implied someone who was too theoretical (I have always prided myself on a high degree of practicality and on my ability to get my "hands dirty"). This was initially a surprise however my new world of opportunity is one that I now much prefer."

The Career Changer

"Little did I realise it at the time, but my decision to pursue a doctorate was one of the most important and formative choices I have ever made. It resulted in a complete career change, a rich and varied intellectual experience and an opportunity to think deeply about an area I had worked in for many years.

The most significant and obvious change was the move from a senior position in banking, where I had been leading a research department, to a position in academia. Such a significant transition often requires a catalyst and, for me, completing the DBA was the bridge to facilitate that change. It introduced me to new people, alternative ways of thinking and novel approaches to research. This latter point was particularly important. Originally, I intended my doctorate to employ a quantitative methodology and use an experiment to analyse the reaction of financial market professionals to different information sets. However, through a process of reading and discussion with my supervisors and others, I ended up employing a qualitative research design. In this process, I came to understand the opportunities provided by embracing subjectivity in research rather than trying to strive for objectivity alone. To grapple with the complexity of real-world problems needs an expansive approach which often entails embracing uncertainty, emotion, irrationality and ultimately, subjectivity.

A doctorate is composed of thousands of steps, some quite significant and others trivial. It is when it is completed that we begin to see the result and can reflect properly on the overall experience. Undoubtedly for me it was a worthwhile and transformational journey."

Discussion and Conclusions

Each of these case studies are unique perspectives from DBA graduates. Each motivation is different, and this results in varied outcomes, both for the individual and the wider context in which they are operating. Although the examples are all different, there are some common themes which emerge.

Development of deep expertise and thought leadership

In several cases, the DBA graduates express a desire to develop a deeper understanding of their area of competency and thereby increase their confidence and credibility. This is expressed by the Olderpreneur who aims to understand the experience of older entrepreneurs. The Executive Coach has developed a strong thought leadership position in the area of trust with a book and a foundation based on the research conducted. The Senior Procurement Director explicitly mentions the desire to test the level of their expertise and that the DBA has legitimised their own credibility and self-confidence to be a thought leader in the field.

The DBA can play a key role in building the confidence of the individual in their own expertise and ability to be a thought leader in a particular field.

Personal transformation

Several of the DBA graduates describe how the DBA has been a transformational experience for them. For example:

"Little did I realise it at the time, but my decision to pursue a doctorate was one of the most important and formative choices I have ever made. ... Undoubtedly for me it was a worthwhile and transformational journey." (The Career Changer).

This transformation is not always and easy process and can be uncomfortable:

"...that I had to revisit and question everything that I thought I knew which was a necessary (but humbling) experience." (Senior Procurement Director).

"At times I felt really uncomfortable and utterly out of my depth." (The Olderpreneur).

Launching of new organisational forms

For several of the DBA graduates, an important outcome of their research has been to launch a new organisational form to promote and disseminate their research, for example:

* A community interest company (the Olderpreneur)
* A foundation (the Executive Coach)
* A blog and thought leadership organisation (the Senior Procurement Director

These case studies illustrate very powerfully how the DBA offers the individual the possibility to transform themselves and their careers; this is what makes the DBA such a rewarding qualification for those who embark on it.

15

DBA as Identity Space

Hendrik S. Kriek, IEDC-Bled School of Management, Bled, Slovenia

This chapter focuses on the DBA as identity space. It addresses how the content of the DBA allows for transformation of personal, relational, collective, professional, and leader identity. The nature of the identity space is discussed as an identity work space, ecological space, archetypical space and, finally, an experimental space. The chapter points to the effect of a DBA as identity space by pointing out how it facilitates personal expression, expands skills, builds social stewardship, creates connections, focuses on connection with candidates' inner worlds, encourages meaning-making and prepares for future identity.

Keywords: Identity, space, effect, identity workspace.

Introduction

Management education scholars increasingly realise that the role of business schools should extend its traditional aims of creating and disseminating knowledge to also play a part in transforming students. This requires scrutiny of participants' understanding of their roles as leaders within organisations and society alike, and should lead to an increased sense of their responsibility to contribute to a better world. In taking up this enhanced responsibility, business schools should emphasise the increasing importance of identity formation as one of its key outcomes. Identity can be seen as a collection of meaning about oneself and perceptions of how others see you. It also includes views on what are appropriate behaviour and how one views oneself in social/other settings. Identity is built and developed in spaces where there is challenge, with stretch and growth often required. Studying towards a DBA allows for such opportunities. Therefore, in this chapter, the focus is on the DBA as identity space.

DBA as identity space

For an identity space to act effectively, it has to allow for tension, discomfort and discontent. Here we limit discussion to show how paradoxes existent in a DBA fit this requirement and may provide the challenge to build, develop and transform identity. Some of these paradoxes include:

Theoretical and/or practical

Any DBA allows for reflection, examination and scrutiny of practical experience against academic and theoretical insights. Whilst these are often complementary, they could allow for paradoxes to be clear where "real-world" experience comes up against theory that may not seem consistent with personal experience.

Personal and/or professional growth

Whether a DBA programme is designed to focus directly on personal development or whether it is assumed that growth happens inadvertently where a programme is more focused on professional growth, it is inevitable that development takes place. This growth happens on both a personal and professional level and these two levels are often in opposition to one another. For example, when an individual's history, aspirations and competencies are examined it may lead to adjusting professional identity.

Personalization and/or contextualization

Personalization is the process through which people "examine their experience and revisit their life story as part and parcel of learning" (Petriglieri, 2011). Contextualization indicates the process through which people examine the needs and aspirations of the groups on whose behalf they lead (Petriglieri & Petriglieri, 2015). When studying towards a DBA, students inevitably examine their contexts, points of view, perspectives and social interactions. For example, the act of being a student "again" or having to answer "why do you do it" requires examination of personal motivations. At the same time, demands from the social context may require one to meet societal demands (e.g., remain part of the "rat race"). Dealing with dilemmas associated with personal versus societal demands may provide opportunity to examine identity.

DBA as *identity* space

Identity involves the constant interplay, interaction and confluence between different components thereof. All these components i.e., personal, relational, collective, professional, and leader identity may be influenced when pursuing a DBA.

Personal identity

Personal identity refers to how an individual defines him or herself and includes beliefs, values, goals, self-esteem, and behavioural manifestations of one's identity. It refers to the sense of "self", pointing to how someone discovers, constructs, shapes, and re-shapes their identities. Embarking on DBA studies can transform and augment one's identity and these changes could provide energy to complete such studies.

Relational identity

Relational identity indicates the co-construction of identities as they exist and evolve within interpersonal spaces. For example, when a DBA candidate takes on the role of "student", "researcher" or "prac-ademic" it enables him or her to expand their roles beyond that of business practitioners because new role-relationships are formed. Thus, working towards and being awarded a DBA may allow for an identity to be discovered, constructed and shaped as the candidate claims an adjusted identity.

Collective identity

The social group or category to which an individual belongs, influences and determines their collective identity. It can be referred to as the individual's social identity as it indicates an individual's sense of who they are, based on their group membership(s). This sense of belonging shapes identity and explains the psychological basis of group behaviour and group association. Doing a DBA allows for a collective identity to be formed as it facilitates belonging to an academic institution, being part of a peer-group and entering the larger academic community.

Professional identity

Adding an identity such as "academic" to existing professional identities requires re-evaluation of existing identities and experimentation with new, potential identitites. This often leads to a decrease in a participant's "original" professional identity where a candidate deconstructs, adjusts and reviews identities he or she no longer finds appropriate. The DBA educational environment allows for experimentation and redefinition that facilitate emergence of a different professional identity that combines professional and academic identities.

Leader identity

Leader identity can be seen as that part of one's identity that "relates to being a leader or how one thinks of oneself as a leader" (Day & Harrison, 2007: 365) and includes "leadership schemas, leadership experience and future representations of oneself as a leader" (Epitropaki et al, 2017: 9). Often DBA candidates are already in leadership positions or expect that the degree will assist them in developing their future leadership aspirations. Therefore, a DBA enables the development of a leader identity that increases in strength, allowing for the meaning attached to leadership identity to be altered, and for integration of different parts of identity into a transformed leader identity.

DBA as identity *space*

For identity to be developed, a context or "space" is needed that facilitates experiences of uncertainty, destabilization, fragmentation, and anxiety. The study context of a DBA is such a space as it offers social feedback that validates and consolidates identity construction. The use of DBA as a space wherein identity can develop, becomes clear when the following opportunities are explored:

Identity work space

Identity workspaces are social settings that are conducive to the development and maintenance of leaders' identities. They build a sense of belonging, facilitate transition into new careers and envisaged futures, and guide transition to a new identity. In the same way as studies help in becoming a DBA graduate, it acts as identity work space because it allows for forming, developing, adjusting and re-imagining of identity.

Ecological space

This space refers to the environment wherein identity development takes place and positions the DBA within larger cultural and societal environments. It indicates how in some instances business schools make deliberate use of their external environment. For example, the IEDC Bled School of Management is located on the banks of the scenic Lake Bled. This brings the environment and education in close proximity and allows for development to take place. In addition, the school is designed to resemble an art gallery with paintings, sculptures and other artefacts to afford students opportunities for reflection, observation, and to contemplate the impact thereof on themselves. This allows for the redefinition and construction of identity.

Archetypal space

Committing to DBA studies confronts participants with the enormity of the task ahead of them. Similar to when someone climbs a mountain and at the top realises how this individual achievement pales against the majesty of nature and the enormity of the surrounds, so too does the individual milestone of doing a DBA constantly reflect against the enormity of the accomplishments of academia through many centuries. This creates an "archetypal space" that allows for a sense of humbleness, awe and for renewed energy to emerge, and creates a space wherein identity work can happen.

Experimental space

Individuals have agency to construct their own identities within the confines of social settings and social construction. When a DBA functions as identity space it offers opportunity where an individual can *experiment* with constructing a new identity. A different identity does not form merely because one is a DBA candidate, or because of membership of a DBA class or institution. It requires active experimentation with how a new identity as DBA graduate could be integrated, enhanced and developed by expanding and adjusting current identities.

Effect of DBA as identity space:

When the effect of the DBA on identity is considered, a number of outcomes can be seen. Among these are the ones the DBA as identity space allows for:

Personal expression

By being an expert and having a deep understanding about a particular topic, DBA graduates are given a voice to articulate their ideas and to disseminate the results of their work. This provides opportunity for them to use the identity to express themselves and to make a contribution to academia, management and practice.

Expansion of skills

The DBA allows for the acquisition of a different set of competencies. Apart from cognitive and technical competencies like academic writing, research methodologies and critical thinking, it allows for more personal competencies to evolve as well. Examples include resilience (e.g., the levels required to complete the programme of study), finding comfort with ambiguity, dealing with the inevitable emotional roller-coaster of doctoral studies, and improved decision-making skills.

Social stewardship

Being a holder of a doctoral degree confers certain levels of responsibility and holding stewardship of what the degree offers within the domain of the academic context. It requires focused behaviour associated with these perceptions and consistent with expectations. This requires expanded views of candidates' identities and allows graduates to operate with adjusted identities.

Connection

The world of academia allows for new connections to open up and the DBA provides an opportunity to leverage such connections. Not only do participants belong to new peer-groups but as candidates and graduates, they connect with the broader academic world. In particular, where opportunities open up to connect with experts and renowned specialists it facilitates identity development – in particular when the DBA facilitates a sense of confidence that one can comfortably interact with experts. Inevitably these lead to an adjustment or redefinition of identity and allow for new roles to emerge.

Connecting the inner world

Being part of a DBA is also a journey that connects individuals with themselves. It allows for personal transformation; increased self-awareness and makes them more confident in the competency and behavioural sets they have acquired. This builds self-confidence, a sense of potency and reinforces identity adjustments.

Meaning-making

Completing a DBA can act as an identity space since it allows for meaning-making to occur. This could be in terms of understanding a particular field of study but also to make sense of how certain processes evolved in an individual, team or organisation, and how it allows for insights into a person's career and/or experience. In offering a different academic lens through which to view the world, this provides new opportunities to make meaning. It goes without saying that it also applies to how individuals find the DBA experience to be meaningful and the subsequent impact thereof on identity.

Future identity

Often a DBA is pursued with a different future in mind and candidates want to use that to reposition their careers, change areas of specialisation, set-up new opportunities or rise in organisational hierarchies. Where the DBA acts as identity space this allows for participants to shape their futures to be aligned with their aspirations and allows for organisations to benefit from transformed contributions.

Conclusion

When a DBA is seen as an identity space, it would appear that the inherent paradoxes in pursuing such a qualification offer fertile ground for transformation to take place. In particular, since different parts of identity including personal-, relational-, collective-, professional-, and leader identity can be adjusted, enhanced and developed while pursuing a DBA. Therefore, the DBA space acts as identity workspace, ecological, archetypical and experimental space. This allows for the impact during the study to be enhanced beyond graduation and models how future development of identity could be enhanced.

16

The DBA as a Game Changer: A Case Study from One Institution

Helen E. Higson and Simon Willans, Aston University, Birmingham, UK.

This chapter explores ways in which a DBA programme can be a significant game-changer to all its stakeholders: business schools, organisations, and students. Based on the literature, we identify the key features of the DBA and how the qualification plays a role in upskilling senior executives, bringing cutting-edge change to companies, and increasing the external impact of business schools. We examine the initiative of one business school to elevate to a new level in the number and quality of their DBA students, allowing us to identify the gains and challenges encountered by the school. We discovered these advantages brought benefits to all parties, well beyond those studying on the DBA. It increased the quality of delivery and supervision for all doctoral students, helped staff build their experience of supervision, and overall changed the level of customer service and professionalism in pastoral support which led to growth in numbers, but also very high satisfaction and retention rates.

Keywords: Partnership, benefit to organisations, upskilling, stakeholders.

Introduction

This chapter explores the ways in which a DBA programme can be a significant game-changer to all its stakeholders. This includes business schools, businesses and other organisations, and students. Our case study demonstrates that the DBA can be a unique way in which all three stakeholders are brought together to their mutual benefit.

A DBA benefits all stakeholders in a manner that the traditional PhD does not. As Bareham et al (2000) say, "Whereas the PhD is aimed at developing professional researchers, the DBA aims to develop researching professionals. Rather than viewing research as an end itself, the new DBAs have placed research at the service of the development of professional practice and the development of professional practitioners." (p.394) The DBA is undertaken by practitioners who are currently embedded in their organisations, and who can use their studies directly to enhance their work. Students, their employers, supervisors, business schools, organisations and wider society benefit because they can all reach places, they might not otherwise experience. Academics, for example, can have access to cutting-edge organisational practice and policy, employers have a gateway into the latest academic research, and the students form the important catalyst in the centre.

The DBA aligns strongly with the mission and objectives of most business schools, in the current higher education climate, where institutions are expected to be excellent in all they do, but also to do good, having a beneficial effect on individuals, organisations and society as a whole (Brink, 2018). The authors have set out in Table 1 the virtuous circle which they believe the DBA can facilitate, because it is the only activity in Higher Education (HE) which covers all aspects of contemporary academic endeavour: high-quality teaching, and high-quality research; exploration of the link between research theory and organisational practice, which in turn makes a difference beyond academia.

Figure 1. Virtuous DBA circle for business schools

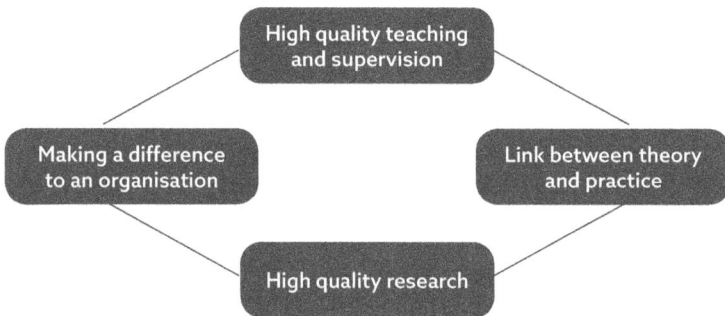

Furthermore, the DBA upskills both the student and the supervisor, academically and professionally. Students develop academic skills to match their high-level hands-on practitioner experience, and they bring a contribution to their companies which creates value-added. They essentially become "researching professionals" cited in Bareham et al (2000) above. Supervisors are helped to remain current with the world of work, and have access to company contacts who benefit not only their teaching but help make their research more relevant and impactful.

Initial work by Breese et al (2021), has indicated that DBA studies have "a wide range of different impacts in the workplace, covering changes to their own practice, wider applications in their organisations/work with clients, producing materials for professional bodies/networks, publishing findings for a wider audience and use in teaching at universities or other education bodies." (p.3) The DBA can also be a game changer for business schools themselves. This is how one business school discovered these benefits.

CASE STUDY

Context

Aston Business School (ABS) is a full range business school, based in Aston University in the heart of the UK midlands. It is situated right in the middle of the country's second city, a place which is known for its contributions to the industrial revolution and manufacturing, but which recently has flourished as a centre for financial, legal, and other professions. The school's origins trace back to Aston University's beginnings in the Birmingham Municipal Technical School, established by the employers of Birmingham who could not find the right skills in 1895. In 1947, the Technical School created a Department of Industrial Administration, the second to be founded in the UK. In 1986 Aston Business School was created.

ABS has had a strong MBA programme for many years, recruiting its first MBA students in 1979, and has recently expanded this to a range of modes: on campus, part-time, Executive, online, and apprenticeship. Despite graduating many MBAs, the School had only run a very small DBA programme (typically no more than eleven students at any time at its maximum), organised as if it was a traditional doctorate. In the 10 years prior to April 2020, a total of 41 DBA students had been recruited. Statistics from the Aston University Graduate School for the years 2016-2022, as set out in Table 2, show the number of applications, offers made, and then the actual starts in each academic year.

Table 2. Yearly DBA recruitment figures

	2016/7	2017/8	2018/9	2019/20*	2020/21	2021/22*
Total Applications	34	51	35	29	111	48
Applications Declined	31	42	30	4	34	10
% Declined	91.18	82.35	85.71	13.79	30.63	20.83
Offers Made	3	9	5	25	77	38
Total Starts	2	9	6	22	63	23

* Single intake

Table 2 highlights a large number of rejections prior to 2019/20. Take up from supervisors was the main driver for this. At this time applications were not channelled effectively to make sure that they were relevant to ABS research areas. If the candidate's proposal was not directly related to an academic's research, the staff member would pass over the application.

What happened to change this?

In late 2016, ABS partnered with a private provider to develop targeted part-time online postgraduate programmes, including the MBA, which could be completed within 2 years. Three years after the online programmes launched, there was a steady recruitment to the MBA of about 100 students annually, across six cohorts. The school had recruited no students in this mode before this. Many students expressed a wish to continue their studies after finding both the online mode of study suited their lifestyle, and that their MBA dissertation topics could be explored further in a way which helped the students' organisations at a strategic level.

ABS's partner carried out market research which highlighted that Aston was one of only three UK universities (along with Cranfield and Reading) with AMBA-accredited DBA programmes that were offered online. At £39,000, Aston is the third most expensive in a competitive set of AMBA and non-AMBA accredited schools (after Cranfield and Manchester) for UK/EU students, and fourth for international students. Most competitors require significant on-campus residencies, which was a barrier to entry to some, and none of the UK competitors offered a programme which was 100% online. So, the Aston Online partnership was extended to include an online DBA, recruiting twice a year, starting in April 2020.'

Results

Within 18 months 108 more DBA students had been recruited and the number of rejected applications had reduced by about 80%. The reduction in rejected applications was due to the different process that was introduced to match supervisors with potential students, and the upskilling and mentoring of staff in the appropriate fields who had not supervised a DBA before. The new programme utilised the existing Aston Online reputation and branding gained from three years of success with postgraduate taught programmes. The school partnered with AMBA, the first partnership of its kind, to promote the DBA programme to a world-wide audience of MBA award-holders. It also promoted the DBA to its own alumni, both on-campus and online graduates, via a targeted scholarship scheme.

Despite the growth, the quality of candidates accepted has not been compromised, and the entry criteria is the same as in previous years. An application, alongside a concise, fully researched proposal is required for initial assessment. If deemed a suitable candidate, a formal interview with both the DBA Directors and a prospective supervisor is arranged who determine the offer to be made. The inclusion of the potential supervisor on the panel also offers the applicant assurances that the University takes their area of research seriously, and that they will be supported from the start if they choose to study with Aston. Feedback from Aston students has shown that this is a competitive advantage over other institutions that sometimes insist on the student finding their own supervisor once they have enrolled.

English language certification seems to be the biggest hurdle for those from non-English speaking countries. Company executives who have operated in business English for years feel offended when asked to take tests, and waivers of regulations to allow them to enrol often take several weeks to approve. This has the potential of delaying an offer and risking losing the applicant to another institution.

Student satisfaction has been very high, and drop-out rates very low. Qualitative comments suggest that this is due to the high level of customer service and student support, as well as the well-thought-out, consistent online delivery. Satisfaction levels over the taught research modules are averaging 4.5 out of a possible 5. Retention rates at 89.6% are also very high; those who have withdrawn have cited funding and job losses as the reason. COVID-19 has clearly changed this both positively and negatively. While we are all more used to working online and virtual study is more attractive, some students reported that their ability to complete the programme was affected by more precarious work lives. Regular contact by both the supervisory and student support teams, ensures that the student is fully engaged and working towards their goals and, in our student survey was found to be a reason cited for reducing the risk of withdrawal. Contact is not limited to active students, as outreach to those on a leave of absence also takes place at regular intervals, helping to transition the student back into their studies effectively.

This has been a game changer in many other ways, well beyond the obvious 900% growth in students. The Research Methods modules for all ABS doctoral students have been improved and professionalised. All materials have been rebuilt to meet the needs of an online audience, a more appropriate curriculum has been introduced, and modules are refreshed again before each delivery. There is a consistency of approach and quality across all modules, based on virtual material and recorded sessions, and regular timed webinars support student engagement throughout the taught element of the programme.

As mentioned above, the new DBA has led to a large increase in staff supervising doctoral students and has also helped to upskill staff members. Student support and backroom processes are much improved, and there is a far greater customer focus. This has enhanced the experience for all our doctoral students, not just those on the DBA, as the better customer service, consistency of taught modules, and increased supervisory confidence of staff have been shared across the school's higher degree offerings. A dedicated DBA programme support officer has been appointed in the central university's graduate school, acting as liaison between the DBA Directors, applicants, and Business School.

Whilst there are two intake points per annum, there is a steady flow of applicants across the year, and applicants are tracked from first enquiry through to offer stage. Application assistance and support from the school's partner enhances what can be done, as they keep regular contact with applicants throughout the application process. The school make the decisions on who to enrol, but the partner ensures the application includes a proposal, references, and personal statements before handing off to Aston. Previously, incomplete applications made it difficult to progress applicants in a timely manner, which did not have a positive impact on potential students.

A maximum of a four-week target turnaround, from receiving application, interviewing, and making an offer or rejecting the candidate, has proven to increase conversions. DBA applicants often apply to many institutions, and those universities that can make a quick offer and show a keen interest appear to win over the applicant, making them feel that their contribution is wanted.

There are now greater connections with industry across the school, and the reputation of the institution since its foundation for excellence and reach in work-based learning has been developed along new lines.

Conclusion

While there is clearly still much research to be done on the impact of the DBA degree on management practice and economic sustainability, it is clear from this case study that there is a market for this form of professional doctorate. Furthermore, it provides a combination of benefits to students, business schools and organisations, which provide lessons for how we design and deliver other higher-level degrees, and how we use both teaching and research to assist our engagement in solving business problems and further developing the management practices of organisations. The DBA is a game-changer because it provides and develops opportunities for research-informed professional development, through the communities of practice and partnership working that Wenger et al. (2002) talk about, but also because it helps business schools to look at their internal processes and procedures in a new way. This brings major benefits across an institution. As a result, students should be confident that it will also be a game changer to their careers.

17

Communication and Dissemination of Impact

Michel Kalika and Stephen Platt, Business Science Institute, Wiltz, Luxembourg[1]

This chapter covers what is widely considered to be a key aspect of DBA programmes, namely the transformation of the doctoral student's experience and tacit knowledge into 'palpable' and 'useful' knowledge for communication and dissemination. This transformation is made possible thanks to the new skills acquired through the DBA research process itself, and the special relationship between the researcher and their thesis supervisor. This newly packaged knowledge, can then be shared with a wider (business) audience in order to generate impact.

Keywords: DBA, dissemination of impact, communication.

Introduction

DBA candidates bring to their programme experience that often goes beyond the 5 years of senior management practice generally required for admission. A 2021 survey of students enrolled at our own institution, showed an average age of 46 years' old with 23 years of post-university business experience. The youngest programme participant was 31, and the most senior 73 years' young and still going strong as an entrepreneur and multiple business owner!

---

[1] This chapter is dedicated to Doctor Mahamat Issein BARDI (1962-2022) group Paris 2017-2020, a practitioner-scholar whose research made a positive impact on the African continent.

When the diversity of student profiles is added to this depth of experience, there is an immensely rich breadth of know-how to be transformed by the DBA process into knowledge that can then be communicated and disseminated to generate impact. For example, Business Science Institute participants come from 50 countries on 5 continents, representing a range of types of organisations -from agricultural cooperatives in West Africa to European management consultancies-, and a breath-taking diversity of job functions and sectors of activity. This inevitably leads to an equally diverse range of thesis topics.

However, the motivations for embarking on a doctoral journey are usually similar from one DBA student to the next, and even across cultures. In "How to Successfully Complete Your DBA?" (2017), Michel Kalika sums up these motivations, as below (adapted).

Table 1: Managers' motivations for pursuing a DBA[2]

Sphere	Motivation	Verbatim
Private	Pleasure	"For pleasure, the pleasure of reflecting, discussing with academics, reading, writing".
	Pride	"I will be proud to publicly defend my DBA thesis in front of my friends and family, and to become a doctor".
	Fulfilment	"Publishing a book about my professional experience is a challenge I want to take on".
Professional	Competitive edge	"Everybody has an MBA in my sector, I need to stand out from the crowd".
	Career Advancement	"To advance my career in an international organisation, having a DBA is essential".
	Legitimacy	"For a consultant, being a doctor is a source of professional legitimacy, and having published the results of one's thesis is a plus".

Source: Adapted from Kalika (2017, p. 27).

---

[2] The examples given in table 1 are specific to Business Science Institute. For example, not all DBAs will be publicly defended, and not all forms of impact will be achieved through the publication of books by participants.

The Creation of impact

The term "impact" is used across a variety of domains, and with different meanings. Research impact has been defined by the UK Research Excellence Framework as 'an effect on, change or benefit to the economy, society, culture, public policy or services, health, the environment or quality of life, beyond academia' (REF3, 2014). In the case of the DBA, impact also includes the personal and professional impact of the thesis process on the researcher themselves as an individual, notably in becoming a "researching professional" (Bareham et al, 2000). Good quality DBA programmes will acknowledge this by embedding impact into the programme design as a process, and not (solely) as an outcome, also helping academic supervisors to acquire the practitioner's tacit knowledge through the shared endeavour and experience of thesis supervision. The overall impact of a DBA process can therefore be illustrated as in Figure 1.

In 2018-19, we questioned 21 DBA graduates about the impact of their DBAs in a series of focus group interviews[4]. Concerning **personal impact,** their responses were clear, emphasising the transformation in others' attitudes towards them, and in their own intellectual growth (ability to embrace multiple perspectives and complexity, development of cognitive frameworks and reasoning processes for problem-solving, and becoming more evidence-based -as opposed to experience-based- in decision making). At the **professional** level, they mentioned

[3] Research Excellence Framework in the UK is the national research assessment exercise, in which impact was first comprehensively assessed.
[4] "What Is the Impact of a Doctorate of Business Administration?" EFMD Doctoral Programme Conference, May 2019, Lancaster, UK (M. Kalika, L. Mola, J. Moscarola, S. Platt).

the increased legitimacy afforded to them after their thesis defence or viva, new career opportunities, changes in career direction, and even, in the case of consultants, the growth in their sales performance!

Figure 1: Approaches to impact

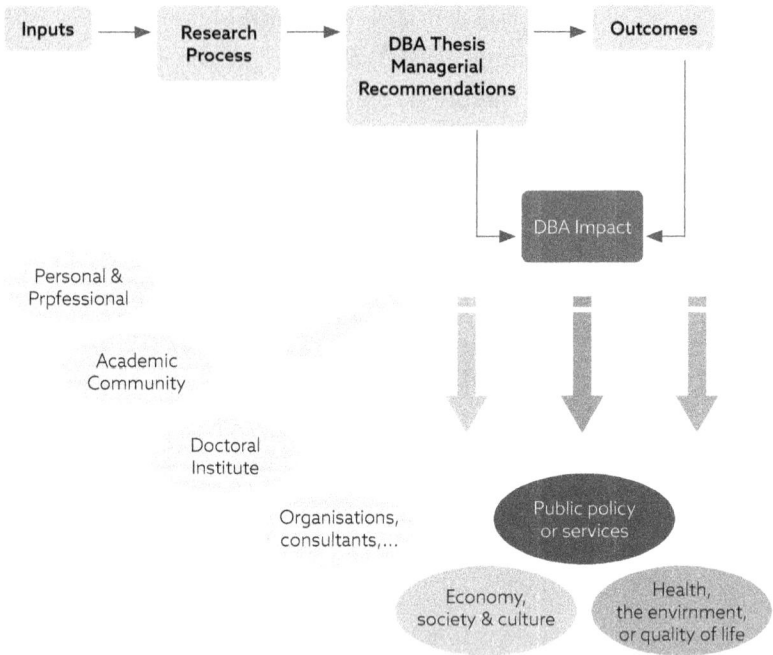

Source: Adapted from Beaulieu and Kalika (2020, p. 145).

When we refer to the impact of a DBA thesis, we are talking about the changes that the graduate generates at the personal level, in organisations, and in society through the knowledge produced. It should also be emphasised that the managerial recommendations in the thesis are at the heart of these changes, and constitute a direct source of impact when they are actually implemented. In the same way, publications that stem from the thesis are a way of communicating research findings and generating academic impact.

Communication and dissemination: generating real-world impact

Impact is sequential, and can take place at **4 points of time** in the DBA research process (Beaulieu and Kalika, 2020) during: **1)** the definition of the DBA project (exchanges between the candidate, professors and other students); **2)** the execution of the DBA project (interactions between the candidate and their organisation/the field); **3)** the dissemination of DBA outputs (e.g. books, professional journals, media broadcasts); **4)** the implementation of managerial or policy recommendations (e.g. development of tools, methods, decision-making processes). It should be noted that points 3 and 4 can also happen in parallel.

Based on our experience, we can illustrate a variety of channels to wider and potentially real-world impact for the DBA research generated initially within the confines of the students *immediate* personal, professional and academic community.

Table 3: Channels to Impact

Channels and examples	Impact target audience	Key DBA student/ graduate benefit
PUBLICATIONS		
Articles in professional journals: *A graduate and owner of a French consultancy co-publishes an article with his supervisor in a Canadian professional journal on a topic related to his thesis topic (negotiations in business takeovers).*	World of practice	Recognition and legitimacy as an expert practitioner.
Books and book chapters: *a graduate publishes a book on her thesis topic (the influence of national cultures on leadership practises in Moroccan firms).*	World of practice and academic community	Personal satisfaction. Recognition and legitimacy as a practitioner-scholar.
Articles in academic journals: *A graduate co-publishes an article with his supervisor in an internationally ranked journal on his thesis topic (adaptive organisational ambidexterity in a Belgian SME).*	Academic community	Recognition and legitimacy as a practitioner-scholar. New opportunities for learning through sustained interaction (socialisation) with supervisor.
CONFERENCES & LECTURING		
Professional conferences: *A graduate whose healthcare consultancy merged with a multinational after completing his DBA, regularly presents papers and posters at international healthcare conferences guided by the research methodology expertise developed during his studies.*	World of practice	Recognition and legitimacy. Increased self-confidence. Interaction and networking. Opportunity to 'test' research findings with other real-word practitioners. Direct impact on business performance.
Academic conferences: *A 1st year student researching 'The place of women in public sector governance in Niger' presents her work at an International Academic Conference on 'Women and Governance' at a French university.*	Academic community	Interaction and networking with academics and practitioners offering feedback and new critical perspectives on research topic. Confidence building in an emerging role as a practitioner-scholar.

Lecturing: *A graduate is offered a position as a part-time lecturer in Information Systems at an American University following his thesis on Mobile Technology Fitness for Mines.*	Students from the world of practice Undergraduate and postgraduate students	Personal satisfaction. Opportunity to self-reflect through teaching, interacting and sharing.

MEDIA

Specialist magazine articles: *A graduate publishes an article in a specialist French real estate magazine on the results of his research on cognitive rent and the uberization of the property market.*	World of practice	Recognition and legitimacy as an expert practitioner.
Public media appearances: *a graduate is invited to a televised presentation of her research findings on the employment and employability of senior citizens.*	World of practice, academia and the general public	Recognition and legitimacy as an expert practitioner.
Specialist media appearances: *A graduate is interviewed to talk about his research on the transformation of public and private hospitals as part of a week-long video series by the national business newspaper.*	World of practice	Recognition and legitimacy
Online media (one-off): *A 2nd year DBA student working in the training department of a multinational co-writes an Op. Ed. in The Conversation with her supervisor on the German apprenticeship system, a topic related to her DBA research (boundary spanning in vocational training units).*	World of practice and academic community	Recognition and legitimacy among peers, clients & prospects
Media partnerships: *via a partnership with XerfiCanal[5] (video broadcasts of academic research to the world of business), selected DBA graduates have a 10-minute slot to present their research findings interviewed by a journalist.*	World of practice and academic community	Recognition and legitimacy (e.g., YouTube views)

---

[5] Please see: https://www.xerficanal.com/ (in French).

Social media / networks, blogs: *a media interview on a graduate's thesis findings (factors for managers choosing employers located in rural German areas) is relayed via LinkedIn, Twitter and YouTube.*	World of practice, academic community and the general public	Recognition and legitimacy among peers, clients & prospects

BUSINESS

Company talk: *a graduate is invited to present his research findings to the Central Bank of West African States on governance and risk management in Malian banks.*	World of practice	Recognition and legitimacy as an expert practitioner.
New business services: *Based on his thesis (negotiations in business takeovers), a graduate consultant develops a bespoke training package for his clients.*	Clients	Recognition and legitimacy among peers, clients & prospects. Improved business performance.
Secondments: *A graduate working for the State of Geneva in Switzerland is seconded to another state department to oversee the implementation of its environmental strategy (his DBA research topic).*	Other organisations	Career progression. Recognition and legitimacy through influence in implementing change.
Consultancy: *Upon completion of his DBA, a graduate (director of a clinic) is offered opportunities for consultancy work in the field of healthcare management based on his thesis topic (private clinic management).*	World of practice	Recognition and legitimacy. Career progression.
Advisory Board: *The same graduate becomes a non-Executive director at the Ministry of Health in Tunisia.*	World of practice	Recognition and legitimacy. Career progression.

OTHER

Miscellaneous in-house initiatives: *focused on alumni research activities or news, e.g., Managerial Impact Award; Impact(s) Journal; Alumni Spring Impact Seminar; Monthly Newsletter; Website; Videos, ...*	DBA academic community, alumni	Recognition and legitimacy.

While this table provides numerous examples of how the expertise of practitioner-scholars can be exploited for wider impact, it is by no means exhaustive nor representative of all DBA providers. Strategies, focuses and resources differ from one institution to the other. Some university DBAs with powerful academic research cultures (and the pressures that go with this) may prefer to encourage their graduates to focus primarily on publishing in academic journals, whereas others without the burden of such pressures, may be able to make alternative strategic choices. In the case of our organisation, we have built opportunities for communication and dissemination of impact into the DBA research process, even including it in our mission and vision statements. It should also be pointed out to potential DBA applicants that AMBA itself requires programmes to be able to demonstrate an explicit focus on impact to at least some degree.

A good albeit very institution-specific example is the Business Science Institute book collection, which in addition to publications by faculty on DBA education, includes books written by graduates on the outputs of their DBA research. Interestingly, the collection also includes 'joint' publications by professors with graduates and current DBA candidates. For example, in 2020 and 2021 two books on the impact of the COVID-19 crisis on management practice were published[6], involving in total 33 professors and 9 graduates across the two projects. As another example of this, at Cranfield School of Management,

---

[6] https://www.editions-ems.fr/livres/collections/business-science-insti-tute.html The Impact of the Crisis on Management Practice (in French). The Sustainable Impact of the Crisis on Management Practice (in French).

it is within the University regulations that all publications by DBA researchers should be joint-authored with their research supervisor.

Impact on supervisors

Such collaborations offer unusually deep levels of impact through the high socialisation between academics and practitioners over time in addition to the actual publishing of the book. Indeed, one of the key characteristics of the DBA is the opportunities it offers academics and managers for mutual learning. Indeed, the interactions, or 'entanglements' (Rigg et al., 2021) between the DBA candidate, their supervisor and members of a cohort represent forms of socialisation (Mitchell et al., 2021) that offer opportunities for experienced practitioner-scholars to share their tacit knowledge for the wider benefit of all.

DBA candidates will indeed find in their supervisor an enthusiastic academic sparring partner, motivated by the prospect of making a contribution to the advancement of management practice, and very aware of the valuable expertise managers bring to this advancement. At a recent faculty meeting, we asked our professors to express their reasons for working on a DBA programme. Motivations included "direct access to the field", "the contextualisation of knowledge", or "the opportunity to learn from my doctoral student". Interestingly, colleagues also talked about a feeling of purpose and identity as management scholars:

"Among the things that can be a source of motivation for us and for our DBA students, of course, is the idea of being

useful in some way and therefore making an impact through our work".[7]

The DBA as a journey

In this short chapter, the DBA journey has been referred to as a process. With regard to impact, this process is just one stage in a longer journey that often continues beyond graduation. Post-DBA perspectives for generating impact are numerous as illustrated in table 3, but our belief is that the doctoral institution itself should play an active role in encouraging alumni to generate impact by offering them structured opportunities for sharing the knowledge produced through their research. Just one example of such an initiative at Business Science Institute includes a 3-year Associate Researcher status for graduates who wish to take their scholarly work further, with free access to academic databases, and opportunities for collaboration with faculty.

Conclusion

Managers bring to DBA programmes valuable sources of tacit knowledge through their experience and know-how. A well-structured research process led by the academic expertise of their supervisor and supported by the doctoral academic institute, will enable this tacit knowledge to be transformed into outputs that go beyond the immediate personal or professional impact of the DBA thesis to create impact that potentially has wider, real-world implications.

---

[7] Translated from French: "Parmi les éléments qui peuvent nous motiver et les doctorants bien entendu, c'est bien sûr l'idée d'être utile à quelque chose et donc d'avoir un impact à travers nos travaux", Alain Burlaud, Emeritus Professor of Management at CNAM, France.

REFERENCES

AMBA. (2016). *DBA Accreditation Criteria.* https://www.associationofmbas.com/

Anderson, L., Gold, J., Stewart, J. & Thorpe, R. (2015). *A guide to professional doctorates in business and management.* Sage.

Banerjee, S. & Morley, C. (2013). Professional Doctorates in Management: Toward a Practice-Based Approach to Doctoral Education. *Academy of Management Learning and Education,* 12(2), 173-193.

Bareham, J., Bourner, T. and Ruggeri Stevens, G. (2000), The DBA: what is it for?. *Career Development International,* 5(7), 394-403.

Bartunek, J. M., & Rynes, S. L. (2014). Academics and Practitioners Are Alike and Unlike: The Paradoxes of Academic–Practitioner Relationships. *Journal of Management,* 40(5), 1181-1201.

Baudet, C. (2021). *Doctors Advising Doctoral Students: study tips for doctoral students from doctoral students* (Editor). Éditions EMS.

Beaulieu, P., & Kalika, M. (2020). *The DBA Thesis Project in Practice.* Éditions EMS.

Bourdieu, P., & Passeron, J.-C. (1990). *Reproduction in Education, Society and Culture,* 2nd ed., Sage.

Breese, R. and Issa, S. and Tresidder, R. (2021), *Impact on Management Practice after Completing the DBA* (October 18, 2021). Proceedings of the Eleventh International Conference on Engaged Management Scholarship- EMS 2021, Available at SSRN: https://ssrn.com/abstract=3944827

Briner, R. B., Denyer, D., & Rousseau, D. M. (2009). Evidence-based management: concept cleanup time? *Academy of Management Perspectives,* 23(4), 19-32.

Brink, C. (2018), *The Soul of the University.* Policy Press.

Chevalier, F., Cloutier, L. M., & Mitev, N. (2019). *Research Methods for the DBA*. Éditions EMS.

Chotiyanon, P., & Joannidès de Lautour, V. (2018). *The Changing Role of the Management Accountants – Becoming a Business Partner*. Springer.

Collins, C., & McBain, R. (2017). Learning the craft: Developing apprentice scholars with the capacity to integrate theory and practice. *In Academic-Practitioner Relationships,* Routledge, 159-177.

Corley, K. G., & Gioia, D. A. (2011). Corley 2011. *Academy of Management Review,* 36(1), 12–32.

Creaton, J., & Anderson, V. (2021). The impact of the professional doctorate on managers' professional practice. *The International Journal of Management Education,* 19(1), 100461.

Day, D. V., & Harrison, M. M. (2007). A multilevel, identity-based approach to leadership development. *Human Resource Management Review,* 17(4), 360–373.

Dinham, S., & Scott, C. (1999). *The Doctorate: Talking about the degree,* University of Western Sydney.

Dweck, A. S. (2006). *Mindset: The New Psychology of Success*. Ballantine Books.

Edmondson, A. (1999). Psychological safety and learning behavior in work teams. *Administrative Science Quarterly*, 44(2), 350-383.

Edmondson, A. C., & Daley, G. (2020). How to foster psychological safety in virtual meetings. *Harvard Business Review, 25.*

Epitropaki, O., Kark, R., Mainemelis, C., & Lord R. G. (2017). Leadership and followership identity processes: A multilevel review. *The Leadership Quarterly,* 28 (1), 104–129.

Fink, D. (2006). Theprofessional doctorate: Its relativity to the PhD and relevance for the knowledge economy. *International Journal of Doctoral Studies,* 1(1), 35-44.

Gall, M. and Pigni, F. (2022), Taking DevOps mainstream:

a critical review and conceptual framework. *European Journal of Information Systems,* 1-20.

Garrison, D. R. (2015). *Thinking Collaboratively: Learning in a community of inquiry.* Routledge.

Garrison, D. R., Anderson, T., & Archer, W. (2010). The first decade of the community of inquiry framework: A retrospective. *The Internet and Higher Education,* 13(1-2), 5-9.

Geirland, J. (1996). Complicate yourself! An interview with Karl Weick. *Wired Magazine.* http://www.wired.com/wired/archive/4.04/weick_pr.html

Gibbons, M., Limoges, C., Nowotny, H., Schwartzman, S., Scott, P., & Trow, M. (1994). *The new production of knowledge: The dynamics of science and research in contemporary societies.* Sage.

Grint, K. (2005). *Leadership: Limits and Possibilities.* Palgrave Macmillan.

HEFCE (2007). *PhD Research Degrees: Update. Entry and Completion.* Higher Education Funding Council for England.

He, W., Goodkind, D., & Kowal, P. R. (2016). *An aging world: 2015. International Population Reports.* https://www.census.gov/content/dam/Census/library/publi- cations/2016/demo/p95-16-1.pdf

Huisman, J., & Naidoo, R. (2006). The Professional Doctorate: from Anglo-Saxon to European Challenges. *Higher Education Management and Policy,* 18(2), 57-69.

Jones, M. (2018). Contemporary trends in professional doctorates. *Studies in Higher Education,* 43(5), 814-825.

Kalika, M. (2000). Le management est mort, vive le e-management ! (Management is finished, long live e-management!), *Revue Française de Gestion,* 129, 80-90.

Kalika, M. (2017). *How to Successfully Complete Your DBA?* Caen, France: EMS éditions.

Kegan, R. (1994). *In Over our Heads; The Mental Demands of Modern Life.* Harvard University Press.

Kegan, R. (2009). What 'form' transforms? A constructive-developmental approach to transformative learning. In K. Illeris (Ed.), *Contemporary theories of learning: learning theorists.... in their own words,* 35-52, Routledge.

Kolb, D. A. (1976). Management and the learning process. *California Management Review, 18*(3), 21-31. http://search.ebscohost.com/login.aspx?direct=true&db=bth&AN=6412409

Kot, F. C., & Hendel, D. D. (2012). Emergence and growth of professional doctorates in the United States, United Kingdom, Canada and Australia: A comparative analysis. *Studies in Higher Education,* 37(3), 345-364.

Lee, A. (2008). How are doctoral students supervised? Concepts of doctoral research supervision. *Studies in Higher Education,* 33(3), 267-281.

Lee, A. (2010). New approaches to doctoral supervision: Implications for educational development. *Educational Developments,* 11(2), 18-23.

Lee, A. (2011). *Successful Research Supervision: Advising Students Doing Research.* Routledge.

Lee, A. (2018). How can we develop supervisors for the modern doctorate? *Studies in Higher Education,* 43(5), 878-890.

Lutz, D. (2009), African Ubuntu Philosophy and Global Management, *Journal of Business Ethics,* 84(3), 313-328.

Malden, H. (1835). *On the origin of universities and academical degrees.* J. Taylor.

Malfoy, J., & Yates, L. (2003). Knowledge in action: Doctoral programmes forging new identities. *Journal of Higher Education Policy and Management,* 25(2), 119-129.

MacLennan, H., Piña, A., & Gibbons, S. (2018). Content analysis of DBA and PhD dissertations in business. *Journal of Education for Business,* 93(4), 149-154.

Madichie, N. O. (2020). Doctoral supervision challenges: What do we know and what can we do about it? *Researcher Education and Development Scholarship Conference,* October 2020, Leeds, UK.

McKenzie, J., & Collins, C. (2020). Transitioning From Expert Practitioner To Apprentice Scholar: Journeys Through Liminality. *British Academy of Management Conference.* url: https://virtual.oxfordabstracts. com/#/event/1520/submission/254

Mederos, L. A. (2021). The Future of Outsourcing: Strategic Outsourcing Controls and the Backsourcing Evolution. *The Future of Outsourcing,* 95-144.

Mitchell, V-W., Harvey, W.S., & Wood, G. (2021). Where does all the 'know-how' go? The role of tacit knowledge in research impact. *Higher Education Research & Development,* 1-15.

Neumann, R. (2005). Doctoral differences: Professional doctorates vs PhDs compared. *Journal of Higher Education Policy and Management,* 27(2), 173-188.

Park, C. (2005). New variant PhD: The changing nature of the doctorate in the UK. *Journal of Higher Education Policy and Management,* 27(2), 189-207.

Peters, M. A. (2019). Ancient centers of higher learning: A bias in the comparative history of the university? *Educational Philosophy and Theory,* 51(11), 1063-1072.

Petriglieri, G. (2011). Identity workspaces for leadership development. In S. Snook, N. Noria, & R. Khurana (Eds.), *The Handbook for Teaching Leadership:* 295-312. Sage.

Petriglieri, G., & Petriglieri, J. L. 2015. Can Business Schools Humanize Leadership? *Academy of Management Learning & Education,* 14(4), 625-647.

Petriglieri, G., & Petriglieri, J. L. (2010). Identity workspaces: The case of business schools. *Academy of Management Learning & Education,* 9, 44-60.

REF. (2019). *Guidance on submissions.* Retrieved from https://www.ref.ac.uk/publications/guidance-on-submissions-201901/

Rigg, C., Ellwood, P., & Anderson, L. (2021). Becoming a Scholarly Management Practitioner - Entanglements between the worlds of practice and scholarship. *The International Journal of Management Education,* 19, 2.

Rittel, H.J., & Webber, M.M. (1973). Dilemmas in a General Theory of Planning. *Policy Sciences,* 4(2), 155-169.

Rousseau, D. M. (2006). Is there such a thing as "evidence-based management? *Academy of Management Review,* 31(2), 256-269.

Schön, D. A. (1983). *The Reflective Practitioner: How Professionals Think in Action,* ser. Harper Torchbooks. Basic Books.

Simpson, R. (1983). *How the PhD came to Britain: A Century of Struggle for Postgraduate Education.* SRHE Monograph 54.

Simpson, C., & Sommer, D. (2016). The Practice of Professional Doctorates: The Case of a U.K.-Based Distance DBA. *Journal of Management Education,* 40(5), 576-594.

Staw, B. M., Sandelands, L. E., & Dutton, J. E. (1981). Threat rigidity effects in organisational behavior: A multilevel analysis. *Administrative Science Quarterly,* 501-524.

Stewart, J. (2015). The DBA and PhD Compared. Anderson, L., Gold, J., Stewart, J. and Thorpe, R. *A Guide to Professional Doctorates in Business and Management,* Sage.

Toffler, A. (1990). *Powershift: Knowledge Wealth and Violence et the Edge of the 21st Century.* Bantam.

Van de Ven, A. H. (2007). *Engaged scholarship: A Guide for Organizational and Social Research.* Oxford University Press on Demand.

Wenger, E. (1999). *Communities of Practice: Learning, Meaning, and Identity.* Cambridge University Press.

Wenger, E., McDermott, R. and Snyder, W.M. (2002). *Cultivating Communities of Practice,* Harvard Business Press.

Author Profiles

Helena Barnard

Professor Helena Barnard is the Director of the Doctoral Programme at GIBS. She is passionate about developing business and management scholars from across Africa and has been able to support 24 doctoral students with grants she secured from the Canadian IDRC and South African DHET. Her research interests are in how knowledge (and with it, technology, organisational practices and innovation) moves between more and less developed countries, particularly in Africa. She researches both organisational mechanisms (notably emerging market multinationals and internet-enabled businesses) and individual mechanisms such as scientific collaborations, the diaspora and doctoral training. The difference between and implications of perceived versus actual competence of entities (whether firms or individuals), the centrality of interpersonal relationships and the ongoing effects of environmental turbulence and instability are *recurring themes in her work. Her research has appeared in the Journal of Management, Journal of International Business Studies, Research Policy, Journal of World Business and others,* and she serves as editor for the *Africa Journal of Management and Journal of International Business Policy.* She was the 2017-2020 AIB Vice President for Administration, is the founding chair of its Shared Interest Group on Emerging Markets and was recognised as the 2018-2019 John Dunning Fellow at the University of Reading.

Claire Collins

Professor Claire Collins, is an Emerita Professor of Leadership at Henley Business School, University of Reading. She is a champion of diversity in all its forms and believes that everyone should feel free and empowered to bring their true selves to any forum in safety and warmth. Claire was the Academic Lead, Army Higher Education Pathway, former Director of Diversity and Inclusion and was Director of the DBA Programme from 2011 until April 2019. She is the co-founder of the Henley Centre for Leadership and served on Senate as well as a number of other key University of Reading committees. She chaired the Women@Reading gender diversity group for six years. Claire's research is in Leadership and Development, Diversity and Inclusion, and Coaching. Her teaching experience includes, Post-Experience, Postgraduate, taught MA and MSc, and Doctoral research, at Henley and at the Rotman School of Management, University of Toronto. Claire has held a number of external examiner positions and also supervises/examines Doctoral candidates. Previous to her work in Higher Education, Claire was a scientist in the NHS and Chief Executive of a set of Family Law Chambers in London. She is now an independent and experienced Executive Coach, Educator and Consultant.

Joy Garfield

Dr Joy Garfield is a Senior Teaching Fellow at Aston Business School, UK. Her subject discipline area is information systems, particularly the early stages of systems development. Joy has a passion for teaching and working towards improving the student experience. With just over 20 years of experience in academia in teaching, research and management, Joy is a Senior Fellow of Advance HE. She has worked at a number of UK universities including the University of Manchester, University of Birmingham, and the University of Worcester. Joy has also been involved with key strategic and curriculum developments through course leadership of a range of undergraduate and postgraduate courses. Research collaborations have led to research not only in learning, teaching and scholarship but also in the requirements engineering and systems modelling disciplines together with interdisciplinary research covering the environment, society and citizenship.

Ruben Guevara

Ruben Guevara has dedicated most of his professional career to research management, and strategic business management. He was regional manager in Latin America at the World Agroforestry Centre (ICRAF), one of 15 global advanced R&D centres of the CGIAR, which is associated with the World Bank; regional manager in Latin America, CGIAR-wide global R&D+i initiative on Alternatives for Slash-and-Burn Agriculture, made up of more than 50 partners and investors worldwide; director general and CEO at the Tropical Agricultural Research and Graduate Education Centre (CATIE), a regional Latin American and the Caribbean R&D+i centre. He was Product Development Manager at the Weyerhaeuser Technology Centre, Weyerhaeuser Company in the US. He was a Board member at the International Centre for Tropical Agriculture (CIAT), a member of the CGIAR; the International Union of Forest Research Organisations (IUFRO), a global network of more than 700 research institutions located in over 100 countries; and at CATIE. He was member of 13 company boards across a range of sectors in different countries. He is one of the main stockholders of two family-owned exporting companies. He joined Centrum PUCP Business School in 2009, as full-time Professor. He was Director of Research. Presently he is Director of Doctoral Programmes, and director of the Centre for Enterprise Studies. He is co-author or co-editor of six books, seven book chapters, and over 40 scientific or technical publications. He has an MSc and PhD in Natural Resource Economics and Management from the University of Idaho in the US, and a postgraduate diploma in strategic business management from Harvard Business School.

Helen Higson

Helen Higson was Provost and Deputy Vice-Chancellor at Aston University until 1st March 2021, a role she held for ten years. She is now Professor of Higher Education Learning and Management in Aston Business School, as well as Associate Dean Accreditations. In this latter role Helen has recently led the School's Bronze Athena SWAN accreditation. Helen is a Principal Fellow of Advance HE, and a National Teaching Fellow. She is a trained Executive Coach, specialising in helping organisations align their workforce, structure, and systems with their strategy. Her recent research, policy and consultancy work includes intercultural training, developing employability and skills development, facilitating a coaching culture, and closing the degree attainment gap. She has supervised a large number of DBA students and mentors other supervisory teams. Helen serves on a range of regional and national boards, including Ravensbourne University London, the Society for Research in Higher Education (SRHE), Winchester College, is Board Chair of Navitas UK Holdings Ltd and the Ikon contemporary art gallery, Birmingham. Helen was awarded an OBE in 2011 for services to Higher Education. In September 2020 she was appointed Vice Lord-Lieutenant of the West Midlands.

Vassili Joannidès de Lautour

Vassili Joannidès de Lautour is the Director of the Grenoble École de Management Doctoral School, an adjunct professor at Queensland University of Technology and the University of Parma. He is an external member of the University of Glasgow Adam Smith Business School exam board. Since 2018, he has been the editor of the Palgrave Studies of Accounting and Finance Practices where DBA alumni can publish works bridging research and practitioner focus. Vassili's research addresses accountability as day-to-day practice and intersects a variety of disciplines: political science, geopolitics, theology, philosophy. His concern is to understand and make sense of field actors' daily activities. Beyond publications in journals such as *Critical Perspectives on Accounting or Accounting, Auditing & Accountability Journal,* Vassili has long been concerned with the social and organisational reach of his research. This has led him to counsel a number of companies, local governments, ministers and former MPs as well as non-profits in France, Australia and New Zealand. This interest in impact has also led him to publish dozens of commentaries in newspapers and practitioners' outlets.

Michel Kalika

Professor Michel Kalika, Emeritus Professor, is the president of Business Science Institute, an international academic network running an AMBA-accredited Executive Doctorate in Business Administration in face-to-face (10 locations) and online formats, in French, English and German. In April 2022, the Business Science Institute DBA programme included 200+ doctoral manager-researchers from 44 countries, 80+ faculty members, 117 graduates, and a collection of 40 books dedicated to DBA studies.

Previously, Michel was professor at iaelyon School of Management, University Jean Moulin, at University Paris Dauphine where he created DBA and MBA programmes, dean of EM Strasbourg Business School, where he merged two business schools, and director of research at Audencia. He is the founder of the BSIS (Business School Impact System EFMD-FNEGE). This process has so far been used in more than 60 Business Schools across 18 countries. A book "BSIS, a decade of impact" is in preparation for publication in 2022. Michel is the author or co-author of more than 25 books (among them "Stratégie" the most frequently reedited French language book in this domain) and approximately one hundred various other publications in the fields of strategy and information technology. During his career, Michel has supervised some 60 PhD students. His research focuses on information overload (the "Millefeuille" theory) and the impact of Business Schools. In 2019, 40 colleagues dedicated a book to him called "Entrepreneur à l'Université", EMS, 307 p.

Drikus Kriek

Hendrik Sebastiaan (Drikus) Kriek is Dean and Director of the Doctoral Programmes at the IEDC-Bled School of Management in Bled, Slovenia and is Associate-Professor of Leadership at IEDC and Wits Business School. He teaches Leadership, Leading High-Performance teams and Organisation Development courses on various Doctoral, MBA and Coaching programmes as well as on executive education programmes both locally and internationally. He acted as Interim Director of the *Central and Eastern European Management Association* in 2018 and was Academic Director of the Academy of Management's Specialized Conference on Responsible Leadership in Dynamic Societies held in Bled in 2019. His latest book, *Team Leadership: Theories, Tools and Techniques* was published in 2019 while the next *"The Art of Leading Teams"* are in press. He studied Clinical Psychology and received his MA (Clin. Psych.) and MBA degrees, both cum laude, from the Rand Afrikaans University (now University of Johannesburg) and the University of Stellenbosch respectively. Drikus received his Doctorate from the University of Pretoria and is a graduate of Yale University in the United States. Drikus consults in the field of Leadership development and had been involved in team development, management education projects, lecturing and leadership development programmes to a variety of local and international organisations.

Jane McKenzie

Professor of Management Knowledge and Learning, Henley Business School, University of Reading **Jane McKenzie** would describe herself as a 'pracademic'. She's happy with the rigour of research demanded by academia and always has an eye to its practical use in improving business practice. Most of her own research has been situated at the interface between academia and practice, particularly within the Henley Forum, which is a community of large organisations and academics focused on improving the use of organisational knowledge and learning to support innovation, organisational development and change. She is particularly interested in the tensions that come from the paradoxical dynamics of complex human and social systems which are always adapting and changing at the same time as retaining mechanism that provide stability and continuity. She supervises many DBA and PhD students, studying in these areas, particularly in the domain of leadership and organisational behaviour. She also teaches research design, philosophy of social sciences and advance qualitative methodology on both programmes at Henley Business School. Before joining Henley Business School in 1997, she worked for 20 years in industry in European financial management roles. She has written four books and many papers. Her most recent book with Professor Jean Bartunek who has written the foreword to this book, examines the benefits, challenges and complexities of academic practitioner relationships.

Michelle Mielly

Michelle Mielly is a development anthropologist and interculturalist with a focus on internationalization. Her work has consistently focused on issues linked to identity, diversity, and community and explores how identity intersects with different organisational and cultural environments. Her research includes work on organisational diversity, migration, post-colonial subjectivity at work, self-initiated expatriates, nomadic entrepreneurs, foreignness and strangeness in organisations, and gender-related questions of leadership & professional mobility. She is a senior editor for HRM and Gender at the International Business Review. Michelle has served as Academic director for various Doctoral and Master's level programmes at GEM including Switzerland, USA, India, and more. Her core teaching expertise is in Intercultural Management, International HRM, Business Ethics, or International Negotiation, and she also teaches courses in Research Methods, Global Work, Expatriation, Gender & Management, Western Intellectual History, Post-Truth & Misinformation, and Leadership. She has published in journals such as *Critical Perspectives on International Business, Career Development International, and Relations Industrielles/Industrial Relations.* Michelle holds degrees from *Southwestern University (B.A.), Université de Grenoble (DEA), Pennsylvania State University (M.A.), and Harvard University (Ph.D.).*

Diego Norena-Chavez

Diego Norena-Chavez is a senior manager, businessman, Professor, researcher, and investor. He is presently Managing Director of Dinor Servicios Generales SAC, and CEO of Stomae Scientific Association. He is also Assistant Professor of strategic management, creativity and research methods at Centrum Catolica Graduate Business School, Pontificia Universidad Católica del Perú, Peru, part-time Professor of research methods at the Peruvian Navy's Professional Specialization School and guest professor at the Peruvian Army War College. Professor Norena-Chavez undertook post-doctoral studies in Management, University of Piraeus, Greece. He is Doctor of Strategic Business Administration, Pontificia Universidad Católica del Perú, Peru; Doctor of Business Administration, Paris School of Business, France; Master of Business Administration, Ramón Llull-Esade University, Spain; Master in Business Administration, Universidad Adolfo Ibañez, Chile; Business Administrator with specialization in human resources, University of Lima, Peru. He is also a Reserve Officer of the Peruvian Army, Peru. He completed the Executive Certificate in Management and Leadership at the Massachusetts Institute of Technology, United States, and graduated from the Senior Management Programme at Incae Business School, Costa Rica. He is the author of two books and ten articles published in Scopus-based journals. He is Chairman of the Board, Vice-Chair of the Board, or Board Member in 15 family-owned companies in Peru.

Chris Owen

Dr Chris Owen is a Senior Teaching Fellow at Aston Business School, Aston University in Birmingham, United Kingdom. He is the course director for the Online MBA programme and also teaches on the Aston DBA programme and supervises DBA students. As a DBA graduate himself, he understands first-hand the challenges and opportunities that these programmes present. Coming to academia from a career in industry and consulting, he also appreciates the boundary spanning nature of the professional doctorate where students have a foot in both camps, the word of practice and academia. Before joining Aston, Chris worked at PwC Consulting with clients across a variety of sectors including banking, aerospace, industrial products, construction, public sector (Home Affairs and Education), utilities and food distribution and has international experience having worked in Germany, Italy, the US and China. His research interests are wide ranging in the area of management science and operations research. From a pedagogical perspective, he is interested in problem based and transformational learning.

Emma Parry

Professor Emma Parry is Professor of Human Resource Management and Head of the Changing World of Work Group. She is a recognised expert in Human Resource Management (HRM) and plays a leading role in a number of global research projects in this area. These include Cranet, a worldwide network of over 40 business schools that conducts comparative HRM research, and 5C, a global research project involving around 30 academic institutions, examining cultural and age differences in attitudes towards careers. Professor Parry's research interests relate to the impact of the changing external context on managing people. In particular, she undertakes research on the influence of technological advancement, age demographics and generational diversity, and national context. Professor Parry has also undertaken a large number of research projects in relation to human capability within defence. Professor Parry is Editor in Chief of the International Journal of Human Resource Management (IJHRM). She is also the Series Editor for the book series The Changing Context of Managing People (Emerald). She is also currently President of the Executive DBA Council (EDBAC), and an elected member of the British Academy of Management (BAM) Council. Professor Parry is a Fellow of the British Academy of Management and an Honorary Fellow for the Institute for Employment Studies, as well as a Visiting Research Fellow at Westminster Business School. She is also an Academic Fellow of the Chartered Institute of Personnel and Development (CIPD). Professor Parry teaches on graduate and executive programmes in the areas of Human Resource Management, Talent Management, Organisational Behaviour and Research Methods.

Stephen Platt

Stephen Platt has an MBA in Higher Education Management from UCL Institute of Education, and has worked in the French education system since 1990 occupying a variety of positions. His company, The Academic Translator, works with Business Schools and Universities to boost their international brand image, translating, copy-editing and writing documents in authentic English. Stephen is also *Expert Associé* at HEADway People, a direct sourcing specialist recruiting exclusively for the higher education, research and training sectors. Much of his time is now spent working as Quality Assurance and Accreditations Manager for the Business Science Institute in Luxembourg, a specialist Executive DBA provider.

Vivienne Spooner

Dr Vivienne Spooner is faculty lead of the MPhil with specialisation in Evidence-Based Management at the Gordon Institute of Business Science (GIBS) of the University of Pretoria, and a long-time member of the GIBS doctoral management team. A proponent of lifelong learning Viv, a late life-stage scholar, has recently completed her PhD in adult education. Her research interest lies in the Scholarship of Teaching and Learning, focusing on how learning happens in post-graduate studies.

Simon Willans

Simon Willans is the Director of Engagement Operations at Aston University and Director of the Aston Online suite of 100% online programmes. He has 8 years of higher education experience and has held several senior roles within both Aston Business School and within the central university, leading and contributing to key strategic projects aimed at enhancing the student experience and widening participation. Prior to working in higher education, Simon spent 15 years as both a project and change manager in the public sector within local government.

Nicky Yates

Dr Nicky Yates is a Senior Lecturer within the Cranfield University Centre for Logistics, Procurement and Supply Chain Management and Director of Doctoral Programmes for Cranfield School of Management. She has a wide general interest in modelling the supply chain and her teaching and research is mainly focused in this area. She teaches modules on supply chain design and modelling, simulation and manufacturing on the Full Time and Executive Masters programmes in Logistics and Supply Chain Management. Her research focusses on simulation and modelling of supply chains from strategic network optimisation to detailed simulation studies. A particular focus of her research relates to the management of supply chains which handle perishable products such as food or blood. She also teaches and supervises across the School of Management doctoral programmes.

Contributing Institutions

Aston Business School
BIRMINGHAM UK

ASTON UNIVERSITY BUSINESS SCHOOL

Aston Business School is part of an elite group of business schools that hold the 'triple-crown' accreditation from AACSB, AMBA and EQUIS, as well as appearing in the top 100 for Business and Management studies (QS World University rankings 2021). Our staff have established a reputation for developing innovative teaching methods to make our students' learning experience more rewarding. Our students experience real-life business activities through placements and initiatives including a module partnership, in-house business clinics, and collaboration with charities. Our departments and research centres work together to further our understanding of key business disciplines and issues, with a focus on innovation and impact. The ethos of impact is built into our study programmes. Our DBA programme is a prime example of this. In particular, the Aston DBA programme is structured for business leaders to build the skills to design and deliver research that makes an impact, strengthen the ability to solve complex business problems, and form an in-depth analysis into a relevant topic and develop a comprehensive research project.

BUSINESS SCIENCE INSTITUTE

BUSINESS SCIENCE INSTITUTE

Business Science Institute is an AMBA-accredited specialist Executive DBA provider, founded in 2012-13 by a group of leading French academics. Business Science Institute is run as an internationally distributed organisation, employing a network of over 100 professors from 45 home institutions representing 14 different nationalities. Our common working languages are English, French and German, with the programme available in 10 locations across 5 continents and online in the 3 languages. This organisation is particularly adapted to the part-time executive status of DBA candidates, and enables the institution to benefit from an international pool of expert resources that identifies strongly with our mission and academic start-up culture. Our programme has been designed to be highly accessible to practitioners whatever their background or context. Diversity is one of the key values of Business Science Institute, and the multi-dimensional nature of our doctoral candidates, supervisors and support staff reflects an open, critical perspective to modern-day management issues. The institution places a special emphasis on developing a research process that supports candidates and faculty in generating real-world impact, whether this be personal, professional or for the good of wider Society.

centrum PUCP ESCUELA PARA LOS BUENOS NEGOCIOS

CENTRUM CATOLICA GRADUATE BUSINESS SCHOOL

CENTRUM Católica is the graduate business school of Pontificia Universidad Católica del Peru (PUCP), a not-for-profit private university located in Lima, Peru. PUCP was founded in 1917. CENTRUM Católica was founded in the year 2000. It offers masters and doctoral degrees, as well as a range of executive education business and management programmes. CENTRUM Católica's purpose is "Educating in business to build a better world". It's mission is "Transforming persons into business agents of change with a positive impact in society". In addition, CENTRUM Católica has a clear mission that differentiates it from competitors "by offering knowledge with a humanistic approach to help students reflect on the meaning they want for their life". The school's approach is enhanced by a strategic positioning as "The school for better businesses" that is embedded across a broad range of activities including an MBA portfolio, specialised Master degrees, Doctoral programmes, as well as executive education. It is ranked as a *Five Palmes of Excellence* Business School by Eduniversal, and has obtained the quadruple crown through accreditations from the three leading international accreditation bodies, namely: AACSB International from the USA, EFMD-EQUIS from Western Europe, and AMBA from the United Kingdom and Northern Ireland. In addition, CENTRUM Católica has achieved the BGA accreditation from AMBA, which recognizes business schools that "share a commitment for responsible management practices and lifelong learning, and are looking to provide positive impact on their students, communities, and the economy as a whole".

CRANFIELD SCHOOL OF MANAGEMENT

As a specialist postgraduate university, **Cranfield** is the largest UK provider of master's-level graduates in engineering and offers a flagship MBA, extensive world-class customised executive education and professional development programmes. Cranfield delivers transformational research, postgraduate education and professional development. Cranfield's distinctive expertise is in our deep understanding of technology and management and how these work together to benefit the world. Our work informs government policy and leads the way in producing cutting edge new technologies and products in partnership with industry. Cranfield School of Management is one of the most internationally recognised and long-established business schools in Europe. As part of Cranfield University, a world-leading, purely postgraduate university, it has been an inspiration to generations of business leaders in technology and management. Our long-standing relationships with some of the most prestigious companies in industry means that we are globally recognised for our excellence in leadership development and real-world focus. Our long-standing relationships with some of the most prestigious companies in industry means that we are globally recognised for our excellence in leadership development and real-world focus.

Gordon Institute of Business Science
University of Pretoria

THE GORDON INSTITUTE OF BUSINESS SCIENCE

Founded in 2000, the University of Pretoria's **Gordon Institute of Business Science** (GIBS) is an internationally accredited business school, based in Johannesburg, South Africa's economic hub. As the business school for business, we focus on general management and aim to significantly improve responsible individual and organisational productivity and performance, in South Africa and our broader African environment, through high-quality business and management education. Our purpose is to inspire exceptional performance in our pursuit to make business healthier. The GIBS Executive Education offering was ranked in the global top 50 by the prestigious Financial Times Executive Education 2020 Ranking. In 2021, the QS World University Rankings ranked GIBS at number 52 for: Global Executive MBA, placing the school's MBA in the top 30% globally. GIBS is the 113th business school worldwide to achieve Triple Crown status, holding EQUIS accreditation from the European Foundation for Management Development (EFMD), as well as accreditation from the Association of MBAs (AMBA), and the Association to Advance Collegiate Schools of Business (AACSB). GIBS is an affiliate of the Central and East European Management Development Association and a United Nations Principles for Responsible Management (PRME) Champion.

For more information, visit www.gibs.co.za

**GRENOBLE
ECOLE DE
MANAGEMENT**
BUSINESS LAB FOR SOCIETY

GRENOBLE ECOLE DE MANAGEMENT

Grenoble Ecole de Management (GEM) is more than just a school. GEM represents an open-ended laboratory – a Business Lab for Society – through which students learn every day to solve complex problems and overcome major challenges for business and society. Founded in Grenoble, a city of science and technology, the school has developed solid expertise in the management of technology and innovation. This foundation has enabled GEM to expand its research, teaching, and expertise to meet challenges in the digital world, healthcare, energy, entrepreneurship, territorial ecosystems in transition, and geopolitics. The Doctorate of Business Administration from GEM is representative of our mission. As a triple-accredited business school (AACSB, AMBA, and EQUIS), Grenoble Ecole de Management has designed and delivered a DBA programme since 1993, thereby being a pioneer institution in Europe. In 2022, it counts 570 graduates bringing impact to their organisation and/or society by leveraging the academic research they have conducted to solve concrete organisational problems.

Henley
Business School
UNIVERSITY OF READING

HENLEY BUSINESS SCHOOL

The Henley DBA programme was one of the first to launch in the UK, in 1992, and contributes to the research excellence of Henley Business School, part of the University of Reading. It is a triple-accredited (AACSB, AMBA and EQUIS), part-time, professional doctoral degree with international scope and reputation, designed to enhance executive and professional practice through the application of rigorous research into real and complex issues in business and management. Henley has international faculty and a community of doctoral supervisors based around the world, with rich academic knowledge and practitioner experience. The Henley DBA enables participants to develop a sound understanding of the conceptual and theoretical underpinnings of their chosen area of research into business and management. Important contributions to knowledge and understanding are made from local business level, through to the wider industry sector and globally. The study programme is designed for international business people, balancing in-person attendance at our stunning campus in the UK with online content and collaboration.

IEDC
Bled School of
Management

Postgraduate Studies

IEDC-BLED SCHOOL OF MANAGEMENT

IEDC was founded in 1986 as the first business school of its type in the CEE, and is today one of the leading international management development institutions in Europe. It is a place where leaders come to learn and reflect, an international centre of excellence in management development, a business meeting point, and a unique place where works of art complement a creative environment for creative leadership. The mission of IEDC, as an agent of change and a learning partner, is to attract the most promising executives and top managers, provide them with world class management education and other relevant services in a truly international context, inspire them for life-long-learning, and prepare them to act and add value as competent and responsible transformational leaders in their organisations and society at large. IEDC strives for education with impact reflected in it being an award-winning institution, accredited by IQA (International Quality Accreditation), AMBA (the Association of MBAs), and NAKVIS (Slovenian Quality Assurance Agency for Higher Education). Along with its highly-ranked International Executive MBA and Doctoral programmes, IEDC offers short executive seminars for senior leaders and a wide range of general management programmes.

www.ingramcontent.com/pod-product-compliance
Lightning Source LLC
Chambersburg PA
CBHW071550210326
41597CB00019B/3184